Capitalism and Democracy

Capitalism and Democracy:
Schumpeter Revisited

Edited by
Richard D. Coe and Charles K. Wilber

UNIVERSITY OF NOTRE DAME PRESS
NOTRE DAME, INDIANA 46556

Library of Congress Cataloging in Publication Data

Main entry under title:

Capitalism and democracy.

Bibliography: p.
1. Schumpeter, Joseph Alois, 1883-1950. Capitalism, socialism, and democracy—Addresses, essays, lectures. 2. Socialism—Addresses, essays, lectures. 3. Capitalism—Addresses, essays, lectures. 4. Democracy—Addresses, essays, lectures. I. Coe, Richard D. II. Wilber, Charles K.
HX72.S383C36 1985 335 84-40362
ISBN 0-268-00750-0
ISBN 0-268-00751-9 (pbk.)

Manufactured in the United States of America

Contents

Preface vii

Contributors ix

Schumpeter Revisited: An Overview 1

Richard D. Coe and Charles K. Wilber

A Critique of *Capitalism, Socialism, and Democracy* 60

Warren J. Samuels

Pressure Groups and Political Behavior 120

Gary S. Becker

State Structures and Political Practices: A Reconsideration of the Liberal Democratic Conception of Politics and Accountability 147

Samuel Bowles

Preface

It is with pride that we at the University of Notre Dame publish this collection of articles in honor of Joseph A. Schumpeter. All the articles are based on or take off from his seminal 1942 work, *Capitalism, Socialism and Democracy*. The early versions of the papers were presented as part of the Department of Economics' New Directions lecture series during the 1981–82 academic year. This is the fifth such volume in the Notre Dame Studies in Political Economy that began in 1976–77.

We are grateful for the enthusiastic participation of our lecture/authors: Gary Becker, Samuel Bowles, Warren Samuels, and Edward Tufte. The last named author's essay could not be included in this volume since it had been, in substantial form, already published. In addition to their formal papers, they spent many, many hours with our students and our colleagues and, in the process, provided fresh insights into the complicated but vital problem of the relationship between economic and political systems.

Without the cooperation of the University of Notre Dame Press and particularly of our editor, Joe Wilder, this volume would not have been possible.

Richard D. Coe
Charles K. Wilber

Preface

[illegible]

Contributors

GARY S. BECKER is University Professor of Economics at the University of Chicago. A prolific author, he has written on a variety of subjects ranging from human capital theory to the economics of crime and of the family.

SAMUEL BOWLES is Professor of Economics at the University of Massachusetts, Amherst. He has written extensively on education in a capitalist economy, liberal democratic theory, and Marxian social theory.

RICHARD D. COE is Associate Professor of Economics at New College, University of South Florida. He is a specialist on government social welfare programs and has published extensively on the food stamp program.

WARREN J. SAMUELS is Professor of Economics at Michigan State University. For many years he was editor of the *Journal of Economic Issues*. He has written on law and economics, institutional economics, economic thought, and a host of other subjects.

CHARLES K. WILBER is Professor of Economics at the University of Notre Dame. He has written on subjects ranging from economic methodology to economic development.

Schumpeter Revisited:
An Overview

Richard D. Coe and Charles K. Wilber

I. INTRODUCTION

A little more than forty years ago Joseph Schumpeter's now classic book *Capitalism, Socialism, and Democracy* was published. The book created an immediate stir, primarily because Schumpeter predicted the eventual demise of capitalism, to be replaced by a socialist economic system. Such a prognosis, coming on the heels of the Great Depression from a renowned mainstream economist, was unsettlingly news to the Western world. But Schumpeter was interested in more than mere predictions concerning the future of capitalism. He intended to present to the reader his view of the true nature of capitalism, socialism, and democracy. These views were often sharply at odds with the prevailing wisdom of his day. It is a mark of his genius that some of these maverick views are now considered the conventional wisdom.

This book is not concerned with all aspects of Schumpeter's thought as presented in *Capitalism, Socialism, and Democracy*. The focus is somewhat narrower. The basic theme concerns the relationship between a capitalist economic system and a democratic political system. This issue, of obvious importance to the Western world, has generated considerable comment. One broad body of thought argues that the two systems are mutually incompatible at the basic philosophical level. A capitalist economic system assigns economic rights (the ability to control resources) according to the principle of one dollar, one vote. Dollars, however, are not necessarily distributed equally across individuals, and in fact are often highly unequally distributed in capitalist economies. A democratic political system assigns political rights according to the principle of one person, one vote, and is thus equalitarian in nature. These two principles are bound to clash, and in the long run cannot co-exist, so the argument goes. The noncapitalist group, which usually comprises the vast majority of the population, will eventually unite and outvote the elite capitalist class, stripping it of its privileged propertied position.

Another body of thought stresses the basic compatibility of capitalism and democracy. Both systems are based on the belief that freedom of individual choice will result in socially desirable outcomes, whether that be in the economic or the political arena. A capitalist market economy relies on the maximizing decisions of individual consumers and producers to achieve an efficient allocation of resources. A democratic political system relies on the decisions of individual voters to achieve the proper resolution of political disputes. In both cases power is widely dispersed. Thus each system reinforces the other. This line of reasoning goes on to argue that a socialist economic system is essentially incompatible with a democratic political system. A socialist economy implies centralized decision making of economic matters, resulting in a concentration of power in the hands of a relatively few people at the top which is inconsistent with the decentralized individual decision making implied by a democratic political system.

Schumpeter held neither of these views, or perhaps more correctly, accepted elements of both. There is indeed a natural affinity between capitalism and democracy. It is not simply a historical accident that the two systems evolved simultaneously from feudal society. However, it is also true that democracy can survive and even thrive in a socialist state. The eventual demise of capitalism which Schumpeter predicted will not necessarily bring with it the end of democracy. His view of the true nature of capitalism and of democracy leads him to these conclusions, and forms the basis of this volume.

This book contains three articles (plus our introduction) by writers who represent various schools of thought in the professional literature. Warren Samuels has long been associated with the institutionalist tradition in economics. Gary Becker is a renowned economist in the neoclassical school; Samuel Bowles is a well-known Marxist. The thoughts of these authors are not all explicitly addressed to the Schumpeterian analysis, but all bear on the question of the relationship between capitalism and democracy.

In this introduction we provide a framework from which to interpret the articles presented in this volume. We begin with a five-part summary of the arguments advanced in *Capitalism, Socialism, and Democracy,* each part covering a major theme developed by Schumpeter.[1] These themes include the nature of capitalism, the question of whether capitalism can survive, the nature of democracy, the relationship between capitalism and democracy, and a brief note on the march into socialism. This summary is followed by a brief outline of the leading schools of contemporary economic thought concerning the relationship of the economic and political spheres. The purpose of this section is to provide the reader with background information concerning the analytical paradigms with which the authors presented in this book are associated. The thoughts of these writers, as presented in their individual articles, are then summarized, followed by a brief comparison of their alternative approaches. The chapter concludes with a discussion of whether the basic themes developed by Schumpeter have been accepted or rejected forty years after their initial appearance.

II. SCHUMPETER REVISITED

A. The Nature of Capitalism

1. The Economic Performance of Capitalism

From his examination of the history of capitalism, one fact stood out clearly to Schumpeter. Capitalism was successful in producing ever-increasing amounts of goods and services. Despite recurrent bouts with recession and regardless of the Great Depression, the capitalist mode of production had resulted in a high sustained growth in the national product unprecedented in history. Furthermore, the fruits of this growth were not limited to any elite class. The incredible productivity of the capitalist engine had enabled the great mass of society to obtain standards of living which were unknown even to kings in the pre-capitalist era. From a strict economic perspective, capitalism was a ringing success.

Why was it so successful? Dismissing arguments that capitalism was blessed by a series of fortuitous circumstances external to the system itself, Schumpeter placed major emphasis on the reward structure of the bourgeois system. In a bourgeois world, money means success, and more money means more success. In a system of "unfettered" capitalism the opportunity is present for the successful entrepreneur to make enormous sums of money. The carrot of "spectacular prizes," combined with the stick of "threats of destitution," is a particularly effective method in calling forth both the productive ability and energy of the business class, as well as providing an automatic regulating mechanism for entry into, success within, and exit out of that class. In short, the profit motive is a powerful incentive to ensure the productive use of society's resources as well as an objective, impersonal measure of the success (or failure) of the individual entrepreneur.

This is, of course, textbook orthodoxy concerning the

function of profits in a competitive capitalist system. But Schumpeter was not a believer in the textbook world of a capitalist economy. Quite the contrary. The textbook view of a competitive capitalist economy paints a picture of numerous small firms impersonally competing in markets over which they individually have no control. The decentralized decision making of these small firms in their quest for profit results in an efficient allocation of resources precisely because no one firm, either individually or collectively, can exert any influence over the market. The Schumpeter world of capitalism, on the other hand, is dominated by large firms which are well aware of the fact that they have considerable control over the market. It is an economy in which the major industries are controlled by either monopolists or, perhaps more likely, a small group of large oligopolistic firms. (Even the relatively decentralized markets are more likely to be characterized by monopolistically competitive firms rather than the conventional "perfectly" competitive firms.) And not only are these large corporations aware of their power in the market, they actively use it. Price fixing, investment in excess capacity to deter potential entry, acquiring control of competing companies are all examples of noncompetitive behavior which Schumpeter would expect to be prevalent in his capitalistic world.

But if this is so, how can Schumpeter argue that the profit motive which propels the entrepreneur will result in a productive use of resources, when any student of introductory economics knows that the monopolist's maximization of profits through restrictive practices results in higher prices and lower output and, thus, in an inefficient allocation of resources? To this question Schumpeter responds with one of his path-breaking ideas—the process of Creative Destruction. How an economic system performs at any given point in time is largely irrelevant. What really matters is how that system performs over time. Dynamic efficiency, rather than static efficiency, is the key to evaluating the performance of an economic system. And this is where "big business" capitalism excels, by virtue of the process of Creative Destruction.

> The fundamental impulse that sets and keeps the capitalist engine in motion comes from the new consumers' goods, the new methods of production or transportation, the new markets, the new forms of industrial organization that capitalist enterprise creates. . . . [These developments] incessantly revolutionize the economic structure *from within*, incessantly destroying the old one, incessantly creating a new one. This process of Creative Destruction is the essential fact about capitalism. (p. 83)

To develop and implement new technological advances requires long-range planning, which will not be undertaken without some certainty that short-term difficulties can be managed. Thus the necessity of big business and the resultant restrictive practices, which provide some insurance against temporary setbacks. And we need not worry about the monopolist becoming complacent behind his restrictive practices, for "the perennial gale of creative destruction" poses a constant threat to even the most established entrepreneur.

This is Schumpeter's conception of "unfettered" capitalism, an evolutionary process which, driven by the bourgeois entrepreneur's desire for the enormous wealth offered by the possibility of engineering the next major technological breakthrough, results in sustained, long-run growth in the output of goods and services. This "unfettered" capitalism is to be distinguished from the competitive capitalism of the economics textbooks, a chaotic and inefficient system (witness the hog-corn cycle) which has little to recommend it. "Unfettered" capitalism is a world in which large-scale industrial concerns—the result of previous successful technological breakthroughs—strive to maintain and improve their position against the onslaught of new technological advances formulated by new entrepreneurs, relatively free from social and political intrusions into their arena of battle. In Schumpeter's view, such a system works and works very well.

2. The Cultural Complement of Capitalism

Schumpeter was not content, however, to view capitalism simply as an economic phenomenon. In fact, it was crucial in assessing the future viability of the capitalist order to recognize that the capitalist mode of production created and continually shaped the social environment in which it operated. "All of the features and achievements of modern civilization are, directly or indirectly, the products of the capitalist process" (p. 125). And the one overriding feature of a capitalist civilization is the spreading of the rationalistic mode of thought. Pre-capitalistic societies were much more amenable to what Schumpeter referred to as "magical" modes of thought, which might be roughly translated as a collective willingness to accept as social truth certain ideas which are basically romantic in nature, particularly in that they are not subject to empirical verification. The belief in the divine right of kings is the archetypical example.

The capitalist system is not sympathetic to such romantic notions. When success is measured by profit, then the successful will be those who can put aside such flights of fancy and keep an unwavering eye on the bottom line. When a fortune is to be lost or made on the next major business decision, one had best marshall all the available facts and reason as logically as possible what the likely outcome will be. An appeal to faith will not convert business losses into profits.

All this sounds very hardhearted and "unheroic," which was precisely Schumpeter's point. The capitalist entrepreneur, relentlessly calculating rates of return and pouring over balance sheets, could become very rich and be recognized as a great success, but stories of his achievements were not the kind to stir the hearts of men or women to impassioned frenzy. Respected and even admired, but not loved—this was the fate of the successful entrepreneur. In one respect, it was probably for the best, for the entrepreneur would not be comfortable bearing the mantle of a legend; after all, he was the nuts and bolts, get-the-job-done person. On the other hand, however, this inability to win the hearts of the people would prove to be a crucial weakness in the capitalist system.

B. Can Capitalism Survive?

We have already noted one of Schumpeter's more innovative contributions to economic thinking—the process of Creative Destruction. He has also been widely acclaimed for his integration of socio-political considerations into the interpretation of economic phenomena, as evidenced by his analysis of the cultural complements of capitalism discussed above. But despite these notable accomplishments Schumpeter is best remembered for his simple two-sentence response to the question posed in the title of this section. "Can capitalism survive? No. I do not think it can." Written while the world was still battling the ravages of the Great Depression, the prediction itself did not distinguish Schumpeter from numerous other observers of the time. It was the remarkable reasoning by which Schumpeter arrived at the conclusion which guaranteed him a place of prominence in the annals of economic thought.

Schumpeter did not think that capitalism would fail on strictly economic grounds. Given room to operate, there was no reason to believe that the capitalist engine could not continue with its impressive record of churning out ever-increasing amounts of goods and services. Popular arguments that vanishing investment opportunities would bring capitalist growth to a halt were dismissed. After all, the secret of the success of capitalism was that it created its own investment opportunities. Schumpeter just did not see anything in the purely economic functioning of the capitalist system which would limit its future success.

But still the system must fail. And if not for economic reasons, then one must look at social reasons. Capitalism's "very success undermines the social institutions which protect it, and 'inevitably' creates conditions in which it will not be able to live . . ." (p. 61). The cultural complements of capitalism—those "notable accomplishments of modern civilization" which owe their existence to the capitalist mode of production—would in the end be the very forces which take the life out of capitalism, while simultaneously laying the groundwork for the "march into socialism."

Schumpeter grouped these erosive cultural forces into two sets—those external to the bourgeois class, that is, those forces which would constrain the entrepreneur from fulfilling his historic role as the driving force behind the capitalist engine; and those forces internal to the bourgeois class, i.e., the forces which would sap the entrepreneur of the desire to fulfill his historic role. We turn our attention first to the external forces, arguably the most crucial to Schumpeter's analysis.

We noted earlier that in Schumpeter's opinion the very essence of capitalism was the process of Creative Destruction, the continual revolutionization of the productive process brought about by new inventions and technological possibilities. The role of the bourgeoisie was to exploit these possibilities, to bring them to fruition. As mentioned above, the incentive to do so was provided by the enormous financial rewards which would accrue to the successful individual entrepreneur. To do this required large-scale monopolistic or oligopolistic business organizations in order to muster the requisite resources and provide for the needed long-range planning horizon. But as the size of the business organization grew, the role of the individual entrepreneur was increasingly usurped by "bureaus and committees." The innovative function of the bourgeois entrepreneur became routinized in the administrative apparatus of the large-scale corporation, run by the salaried manager rather than the individual risk-taker whose livelihood was at stake. And, most crucially, such a system could work. The individual entrepreneur—and the bourgeoisie which owed its existence to his efforts—was not needed in order to maintain economic progress.

> Since capitalist enterprise, by its very achievements, tends to automatize progress, we conclude that it tends to make itself superfluous. (p. 134)

The raison d'être of the bourgeoisie was being destroyed by the evolution of the capitalist system. And in a rationalistic world an upper class without a reason for existing would eventually cease to exist.

There was no shortage of people to point out the fact that the bourgeois entrepreneur was becoming increasingly superfluous. Schumpeter was well aware of the fact that capitalist progress imposed short-run costs on society. Recurring bouts of unemployment were inevitable during the long-run development of the capitalist system (Schumpeter was, after all, an expert on business cycles). The disastrous consequences to individual workers resulting from the temporary slowdown of the capitalist engine was a continual source of social unrest. The most inviting victim upon which to focus this unrest was the bourgeois entrepreneur. Unloved to begin with, he was an easy target for the attacks of politicians and disgruntled intellectuals seeking to win the favor of the masses. Never having much affinity for political affairs, the bourgeoisie was virtually defenseless against such assaults. The one group which in the past might have rallied to the cause of the bourgeoisie—small producers and independent traders—had been swept away in the relentless wake of the evolution of the capitalist system to "big business" capitalism.

> But without protection by some non-bourgeois group, the bourgeois is politically helpless and unable not only to lead its nation but even to take care of its particular class interest. (p. 138)

As if these external attacks on the bourgeoisie were not enough, Schumpeter also believed that the spirit of the bourgeoisie was disintegrating from within. The individual identity of the entrepreneur with business success or failure was disappearing as the family business empire was transformed into the modern public corporation, the result of capitalist evolution. Not that the bourgeoisie minded this process, for who cares about maintaining a family empire if one no longer cares about having a family? In a rationalistic, individualistic utilitarian world, the high cost of raising children provides an increasing disincentive to such activity, especially as children become less valuable as economic assets. Schumpeter foresaw (correctly, it appears) a movement toward childless marriages, particularly in the upper class. And if one has no children, why accumulate profits and build an industrial dynasty? To whom would one leave it? In short, the family home, which Schumpeter saw as the mainspring of the bourgeoisie profit motive, was gradually eroding, again a result of capitalist evolution. Not only did the bourgeoisie no longer have a reason for existence in the eyes of the rest of society, it no longer had a reason for existence in its own eyes.

Thus capitalism will fade away, according to Schumpeter. In his own words:

> Thus the same economic process that undermines the position of the bourgeoisie by decreasing the importance of the functions of entrepreneurs and capitalists, by breaking up protective strata and institutions, by creating an atmosphere of hostility, also decomposes the motor forces of capitalism from within. Nothing else shows so well that the capitalist order not only rests on props made of extra-capitalist material but also derives its energy from extra-capitalist patterns of behavior which at the same time it is bound to destroy. (pp. 161-162)

Capitalism will not crash to its death; rather, it will experience gradual disintegration. And the same forces which cause this disintegration lay the foundation for the succeeding socioeconomic system. That, of course, is socialism.

C. The Nature of Democracy

As the title *Capitalism, Socialism, and Democracy* would indicate, Schumpeter was concerned about how the political system of democracy fit into his analysis. The motivation behind such a concern appears to have been to demonstrate that the transformation of capitalism into socialism did not necessarily imply an end to a democratic political process, a fear often expressed by critics of socialism. In other words, the basic thrust of his analysis of democracy was to establish the point that socialism and democracy were not necessarily incompatible.

In order to establish this proposition Schumpeter first had to disabuse his audience of certain myths which obscured the true nature of a democratic system of government. These myths were the heart of the classical doctrine of democracy. Schumpeter defined the classical doctrine of democracy as follows:

> The democratic method is that institutional arrangement for arriving at political decisions which realizes the common good by making the people itself decide issues through the election of individuals who are to assemble in order to carry out its will. (p. 250)

In Schumpeter's view this definition simply was not adequate to provide an accurate assessment of the actual working of a democratic system. In the first place, it assumed there was a "common good" recognized by all. But people disagree on what is "best" for society—even intelligent, informed people with no special interest to advocate. The concept of the common good assumed there was some overriding truth or ideal which all would recognize and accept if sufficiently educated, a dubious proposition. Furthermore, even if people could agree on what the common good was, there would still exist considerable differences about how best to achieve the desired end.

But perhaps the most serious flaw of the classical doctrine was that it assumed there was "a will of the people." In the classical world, political principles and policies were formed at the grass-roots level and flowed upward to the political leaders at the top. Individual citizens pondered the wide range of issues facing society, rationally decided what were the appropriate policies for these various issues, and transmitted such decisions to their political representatives, who were then to implement the policies. In Schumpeter's view, this doctrine overlooked the most important feature of the political process, which was not to accept and follow but to shape and guide the "will of the people." While individual citizens can be expected to have little difficulty rationally deciding issues concerning their private matters of interest, this is much less likely with respect to issues outside their private sphere, such as international affairs. With respect to these less personal issues, which presumably are the most important ones facing the nation, it is the role of the elected representatives to provide leadership in fashioning the will of the people. The will of the people does not flow from the bottom up; rather, for the most important issues, it flows from the top down. "The will of the people is the *product* and not the motive power of the political process" (emphasis added) (p. 263).

Thus, the classical doctrine of democracy was seriously deficient in providing an understanding of the democratic process. What, then, was the true nature of democracy? The essence of the democratic system was rooted in its unique way of selecting (and replacing) the people who were to have political power. In a democracy, would-be leaders had to compete for the votes of the people.

> The democratic method is that institutional arrangement for arriving at political decisions in which individuals acquire the power to decide by means of a competitive struggle for the people's vote. (p. 269)

To be truly democratic the competition for political leadership must be open to all, and the people must be free to vote for whomever they choose. The winner, of course, is the person (or party) who receives the most votes.

> The principle of democracy then merely means that the reins of government should be handed to those who command more support than do any of the competing individuals or teams. (p. 273)

Democracy, then, is seen as a system in which the people, through their vote, have the ultimate authority in selecting and replacing the leaders of government. No royal succession; no military selection of a civilian ruler; no politburo selecting a one-party slate of candidates to be voted on by the people. The successful politician is the one who can put together a platform on various issues (some of which he creates himself) which appeals to more people than his rival's platform. While politicians are motivated primarily by their self-interest in being elected and controlling the government, Schumpeter believed that they could still achieve socially desirable ends, just as the self-interested profit motivation in the economic sphere would, in a competitive market system, result in the socially efficient allocation of resources. While not interested in the social good per se, if a politician hoped to be elected he would have to develop programs which were considered beneficial by a sufficiently large number of voters. This would ensure that such programs were not uncorrelated with the social good.

Not that the system was without its dangers. In particular, Schumpeter stressed that there would be a natural tendency in a democracy to appeal to voters' short-term interests to the neglect of longer-run concerns. If this tendency were not controlled, the democratic system would not produce satisfactory results, for no system can be successful in the long run without some attention to long-run interest. Schumpeter listed several conditions which a democratic system would have to meet in order to successfully resist this potential danger. At this point we wish merely to enumerate these conditions, reserving for the next section the discussion of how well the capitalist system fulfills these conditions.

In the first place, in order to be successful the democratic system must be able to draw forth a sufficient number of high-quality politicians. Being a politician is a vocation and, like any vocation, requires certain skills in order to be performed successfully. If democracy cannot call forth skilled politicians, it cannot function efficiently. Secondly, in a democracy the effective range of political decisions cannot be extended too far. There is a whole range of governmental decisions which are best left to the experts and technicians rather than determined by the short-run concerns of the electorate. A related requirement for the successful functioning of a democratic system is that there exist a well-trained, respected bureaucracy which can insulate itself from short-term public whims. If a wide range of government decisions must be kept out of the hands of the politicians, there must exist a body capable of intelligently handling these decisions, even to the point of educating elected officials concerning the proper course of action. A fourth condition for the successful working of democracy is that there exist a sufficient amount of what Schumpeter called "Democratic Self-Control." People must have faith that the democratic system can work—that the governments it produces will function reasonably well. If the people become disillusioned with the effectiveness of democratic government, they can, after all, vote it away. (Hitler, it will be recalled, was democratically elected.) By "Democratic Self-Control" Schumpeter appears to mean that the people should have patience with the governments it elects and should not be poised to pounce on every mistake which the government makes. In other words, governments should be given an opportunity to carry out their programs and should not be subject to constant harsh criticism which erodes their authority to govern. This requires voluntary restraint on the part of the electorate and opposing political parties in their attacks on the elected government. Finally, if the democratic system is to function in a successful manner there must be within society a large tolerance for differences of opinion. If political leadership is to be open to all, at least potentially, then people must feel relatively free in expressing their views of appropriate government policy. A necessary condition for the existence of such tolerance is general agreement on the basic "structural principles" of society, which include the fundamental principles which underlie the organization of the economy. In other words, a large tolerance for differences of opinion will exist if the differences of opinion are not large.

We list these conditions in order to lay the groundwork for analyzing the relationship between capitalism and democracy. Can a capitalist economic system fulfill these necessary conditions for the successful functioning of democracy? If so, will democracy protect capitalism from the march into socialism? If not, where does capitalism fail? It is to these questions that we now turn.

D. Democracy and Capitalism

From a writer who was acutely concerned with the relationship of social-political forces to the capitalist economic system, one might have expected a detailed analysis of the relationship between capitalism and democracy. Schumpeter was not so obliging. As noted in the previous section, the primary thrust of Schumpeter's analysis of democracy was to establish that socialism was not necessarily incompatible with democracy, despite a large body of historical evidence to the contrary. His discussion which explicitly is addressed to the relation between democracy and capitalism covers a total of two pages (see pages 296 - 298). Fortunately, Schumpeter drops enough hints before reaching this point to allow some conclusions to be drawn concerning the interaction between a capitalist economic system and a democratic political system.

It is clear that Schumpeter believed that the rise of the capitalist economic system provided a fertile bed for the flowering of democracy. "Historically, the modern democracy rose along with capitalism, and in causal connection with it" (p. 296). And again, "Whatever democracy there was . . . developed historically in the wake of both modern and ancient capitalism" (p. 129). And, finally, "[M]odern democracy is a product of the capitalist process." (p. 297)

What is the causal connection between the two? The capitalist economic system places great faith in individual initiative (particularly that of the bourgeoisie). The economic fortunes of society are entrusted to the rational, utilitarian calculations of the individual entrepreneur. Democracy is the mirror-image of this philosophy reflected in the political sphere. The political fortunes of society are entrusted to the rational calculations of the individual voter. Freedom of individual choice was the underlying motive power of both systems. Once capitalism began to demonstrate in the economic realm that substantial rewards could be reaped from a reliance on freedom of individual choice and initiative, the move to capture similar returns in the political sphere could not be far behind. This was particularly true when such returns promised to be especially high for the emerging bourgeoisie class.

In addition to the similarities in the underlying philosophical foundations of the two systems, capitalism also fulfilled more than adequately most of the conditions necessary for the successful workings of democracy. In particular, the capitalist system has "a solution that is peculiar to it" for limiting the sphere of political decision making. This, of course, is the concept of the laissez-faire, or "night watchman," state. In this view, the government has a relatively limited role to perform, that role being to protect private property rights and individual freedom, primarily by providing for national defense, maintaining domestic law and order, and enforcing contracts. With public functions thus narrowly defined, the sphere of political decision making is consequently limited. And with a limited state it is naturally easier to practice Democratic Self-Control, because there is less government activity to criticize. Put differently, when the public activities are less likely to affect the individual interests of citizens (and the bourgeoisie class), but are directed more toward national issues such as defense, it is easier to exhibit self-restraint and allow the government's policies a chance to work. The threat to the individual of a misconceived policy appears less immediately threatening. A capitalist economic system led by the bourgeois entrepreneur also will display a great deal of tolerance for differing political opinions. The bourgeoisie, primarily concerned with their private business affairs, simply do not care much about various political ideas, as long, of course, as their own interests are not threatened, a condition which will be ensured as long as the laissez-faire concept of the state predominates. And, finally, as the capitalist system works its magic to produce increasing standards of living, a consequence will be an increasingly well-educated populace. This provides an ample pool of talent from which the state can draw to run its bureaucracy, thus allowing for an efficient and intelligent operation of the government.

Thus the capitalist economic system provides an extremely healthy environment in which the democratic system of government can flourish. Yet despite the obvious compatibility between the two systems, Schumpeter did not believe that democracy would prove to be a roadblock for the march into socialism. Capitalism would not find a savior in democracy. The competitive struggle for the people's vote is just that—it's a struggle and it's competitive. Such a system saves only those who save themselves. This requires diligent attention by professional politicians (not simply successful businessmen doing an occasional tour of public duty) to protect one's interest against continued assault by opposing political groups. Unfortunately for capitalism, it is a game at which the bourgeoisie is not particularly adept.

> [B]ourgeoisie society signally failed to fulfill another condition for making the democratic method function. The bourgeoisie produced individuals who made a success at political leadership upon entering a political class of non-bourgeoisie origin, but it did not produce a successful political stratum on its own. . . . (p. 298)

As we have seen before, the bourgeoisie by its nature is not inclined toward political activities, being preoccupied with affairs of business. Their view of politics can be summed up in the phrase "less is better." This natural disinclination toward politics results in a forfeiture of political leadership to other class interests. Without a political leadership to articulate the interest of the bourgeoisie class, the democratic process will not protect that interest.

The remainder of the argument covers territory already traversed. As the capitalist system evolves into "big business" capitalism, the innovative function of the bourgeois entrepreneur becomes routinized, rendering the entrepreneur economically superfluous. No longer serving any useful purpose, the bourgeoisie is an easy victim to blame for the difficulties with programs that infringe on the power of the bourgeoisie. With no political leadership to protect its interest, the position of the bourgeoisie is slowly but steadily eroded, and the capitalist system erodes away with it. Democracy, however, remains.[2]

E. The March into Socialism

Although not germane to the basic theme of this book, it seems appropriate to conclude this overview of Schumpeter's thought with a very brief summary of his vision of the future. The very forces which Schumpeter saw eroding the foundations of capitalism were simultaneously laying the groundwork for socialism as the succeeding economic system. In particular, the transformation of the innovative function from one performed by the individual entrepreneur to one directed by management committees allowed for a relatively painless transition (economically) from capitalism to socialism. The corporate bureaucracy could operate equally as efficiently under the loose guidance of government officials as it could under the loose guidance of the amorphous mass of public stockholders which owned and allegedly controlled the modern capitalist corporation. The adjective "loose" should be emphasized, for Schumpeter clearly saw the potential danger arising from elected politicians interfering with basic business decisions. This problem could be solved in a socialist state if the direct influence of elected officials in the management of formerly private corporations was limited. This could be accomplished by assigning the task to a group of technically trained, independent government bureaucrats, along the lines of our current regulatory agencies such as the Federal Communications Commission. Being under public control did not necessarily mean being under the direct control of elected politicians. All this was a big if, with no guarantee that such an arrangement would actually be implemented. But at least Schumpeter held out guarded hope that the inevitable ascendancy of the socialist state did not spell economic disaster for the advanced industrial economies. In response to his own question "Can socialism work?", Schumpeter responded, "Of course it can."

III. CONTEMPORARY VIEWS OF THE RELATIONSHIP BETWEEN THE POLITICAL AND ECONOMIC SPHERES

A. Introduction

With this broad review of Schumpeter's analysis as a background, we are ready to turn to the thoughts of the writers whose works appear in this volume. Before doing so, however, it may prove useful to briefly review contemporary economic thought concerning the relationship between the economic and political systems. We divide such thought into four schools. The first is the conventional neoclassical normative theory of the appropriate role of the state in economic affairs, a theory which has had such a pervasive influence on the economics profession. None of the writers in this volume, it might be noted, reflect this viewpoint. The other three schools of thought discussed below are the neoclassical positive theory of the state, the Marxian theory of the state, and the institutionalist analysis of the role of the state, each of which reflects the tradition from which one of the writers in this volume emerges.

B. The Neoclassical Normative Theory of the State

Neoclassical normative theory asks the question "What is the appropriate role for the government in the economy?" Phrased differently, the issue is what *should* the government do with respect to economic affairs. Three basic goals for government action are postulated: the government should attempt to secure an efficient allocation of resources, it should ensure an equitable distribution of goods and services, and it should maintain stability in the economy, i.e., it should aim for full employment, price stability, and adequate growth.

With respect to efficiency considerations, the theory revolves around the issue of the legitimacy of government intervention in the private economy. That is, the theory develops a set of principles which enable a determination of when it is appropriate for the government to intervene in the competitive market economy in order to achieve an efficient allocation of resources. This may strike one as an approach which begins with a strong bias against government action. Indeed it may, but it is a bias not without theoretical justification. The starting point of the neoclassical normative theory (with regard to an efficient allocation of resources) is to derive a set of conditions necessary to achieve a Pareto efficient allocation of resources,[3] and then to demonstrate that a competitive market will fulfill these conditions. Having established this, the analysis then focuses on identifying under what conditions this proposition will not hold, that is, under what conditions a competitive market system will not result in an efficient allocation of resources. The conventional analysis classifies these technical market failures as pure public goods, externalities, and natural monopolies. Having shown that in these cases a competitive market system will not achieve efficiency, the implication is that government intervention is then necessary in order to bring about Pareto efficiency. This intervention can take several forms— direct government provision of a particular good or service, a set of government-imposed taxes and subsidies to correct market distortions, or government regulation to alter market imperfections. Other than this, the government's role is to "referee" the competitive market process, primarily by enforcing private contractual transactions and by ensuring that competitive market conditions are maintained.

Does a competitive market system imply a capitalist economic system, defined as the private ownership of the means of production? From a purely theoretical standpoint, not necessarily. Market socialists have long argued that a market system can be employed in a socialist state, thus achieving an efficient allocation of resources while simultaneously eliminating the purported disadvantages of private ownership of the means of production. But despite this, it seems fair to say that the concept of a competitive market economy has been associated closely with a capitalist economic system. Perhaps the primary reason for this is the historical correlation between market systems and capitalist economies, combined with the fact that socialist societies in the past have not been particularly inclined to implement market-type economic arrangements. In any event, the prevailing view of a competitive market economy is one in which private individuals own the productive resources of the economy, which include both human and physical capital. These resources are supplied by the individual in the various markets for inputs into the productive process. These markets will determine the prices which these resources will command, and in turn these prices will determine the incomes of the owners of the resources.

The neoclassical normative theory of the state does recognize that if society does not consider this market-determined distribution of income to be equitable, then it is appropriate for the government to alter this distribution. The theory does *not* attempt to determine what is the most equitable distribution of income. It simply establishes the rather obvious proposition that if one does not believe that the market-determined distribution of income is morally acceptable, then government intervention is necessary to bring about the desired distribution. In the pure theory, the desired distribution is brought about by a set of "lump-sum" taxes and transfers. These taxes and transfers are "lump-sum" in the sense that they do not distort the conditions necessary to achieve a Pareto efficient allocation of resources. If lump-sum redistributions are not possible, the theory then centers on determining the "optimal" set of taxes and transfers, "optimal" in that they achieve the desired redistribution of income and/or endowments with the minimum loss of efficiency.

Finally, there is the macroeconomic role of the government—that of maintaining full employment, price stability, and adequate growth. Since the days of the Great Depression and John Maynard Keynes's *General Theory,* the proposition that a competitive market economy may experience conditions of high unemployment, stagnant growth, or high inflation has been widely accepted. Utilizing the tools of monetary and fiscal policy the government's role is to stabilize these cyclical swings in the economy. Although there is considerable disagreement concerning the degree to which the government should attempt to fine tune the economy, what the appropriate mix of fiscal and monetary policy should be, and whether all three goals can be achieved simultaneously, there are few economists who would argue that the government has no macroeconomic role to play whatsoever.

As this brief overview of the neoclassical normative theory of the state illustrates, the conventional approach of economics toward government focuses on the appropriate functions of the public sector. Notably absent from the discussion above is what role the political system in general, and democracy in particular, fulfill within this framework. Broadly speaking, the role of the political system is to provide policy makers with the information about individuals' preferences which is required in order for the government to carry out its function. With respect to activities which exhibit the characteristics of pure public goods, externalities, or natural monopolies, policy makers must know what individual preferences (i.e., demand curves) are for these activities in order to determine the efficient level of provision. With regard to distributional issues, the role of the political system is to inform the policy maker what society considers to be an equitable distribution of income. With this information, the policy maker can then implement the appropriate policies to bring about such distribution. The situation with respect to the macroeconomic role of the government is somewhat different. Presumably everyone is in favor of full employment, price stability, and growth.[4] If so, the policy maker needs no guide from the political system as to the appropriate policies to implement to achieve these goals. He or she simply has to be well-trained in macroeconomics. However, under the assumption that there exists a trade-off between these goals, in particular between full employment and price stability, the role of the political system is to inform the policy maker of the society's preferences regarding this trade-off. Knowing this, the policy maker can then implement the appropriate fiscal and monetary policies to achieve the desired combination of unemployment and inflation.

In sum, then, the role of the political system in the neoclassical normative theory is to reveal to the policy maker individual preferences relevant to the activities of the government. How does the political system do this? Frankly, this was not an issue with which the theory much concerned itself. This was a problem for the political scientist, not the economist. The neoclassical normative theory did not dictate any particular political system. A benevolent dictator who was well attuned to the desires of the people could presumably fulfill this role.

Of course, the economics profession was not unaware of the fact that democracy was a well-entrenched philosophy in the political thought of the Western world. Recognizing this, the neoclassical normative theorist could point out that the classical theory of democracy was clearly not incompatible with the role assigned to the political system, and in fact, was particularly well suited to fulfilling such a role. In the classical vision, it will be recalled, a democratic political system served as a mechanism for the expression of the "will of the people." If this were so, then was not democracy the ideal political system for revealing society's preferences with regard to distributional issues, the demand for public goods, and the appropriate trade-off between macroeconomic goals? Democracy's political purpose of providing a statement of the will of the people with regard to the common good corresponded nicely with the economist's search for a political system which revealed the preferences of the individual members of society.

In this manner an intellectual marriage between democracy and neoclassical normative economics can be performed. Neoclassical normative theory defined the proper role of the government in the economy, and the democratic political system provided the requisite information for policy makers to implement the appropriate policies. And it seems fair to say that until recently this union of economic and political thought was considered reasonably satisfactory. Not that there weren't early signs of marital discord. In 1951 Kenneth Arrow published his book *Social Choice and Individual Values*[5] which demonstrated that democratic majority rule could not guarantee consistent policy outcomes. In 1957 Anthony Downs published *An Economic Theory of Democracy*[6] which attacked the fundamental assumptions of the classical theory of democracy. But it was not until the 1970s that the full fruition of these initial seeds of discord burst upon the economic profession with the rapid development of what was virtually an entire new field of economic theory—the field of positive public choice.

C. Positive Public Choice: The Neoclassical Positive Approach

The field of positive public choice addresses the question of how governments actually function in society rather than how they should function in some idealized framework. The basic starting point of public choice analysis is the assumption that in making political decisions the participants in the political process—voters, elected officials, bureaucrats—are motivated by the same goal that is assumed to motivate individuals in making economic decisions. That goal, of course, is the maximization of individual utility. In the neoclassical normative theory, policy makers were public servants in the true sense of the word—that is, they were totally subservient to the preferences of the general public. Positive public choice theory rejects as naive and unrealistic this conception of the policy maker. Political actors, including policy makers, have their own individual preference functions which they rationally seek to maximize when operating in the political sphere. Besides representing (at least arguably) a more accurate portrayal of the motivation of political actors, this assumption also places the public choice field firmly within the mainstream of neoclassical analysis of individual behavior.

The public choice theorist takes us into the world of realpolitik. In a representative democracy the individual citizen votes for the candidate whose package of policies offers the highest net benefit to the individual rather than the candidate whose vision of the "common good" most closely corresponds to that of the citizen. (This is assuming that the individual citizen votes at all, the decision on whether to vote also being subject to the utility-maximization calculus.) Political parties and individual candidates attempt to assemble a policy package which maximizes the probability of winning the election, which in general means attracting more votes than any of the opposing candidates. Given that citizens vote their self-interest, then naturally the candidate's platform must appeal to the self-interest of the voter. If elected, the power of government is employed to maintain the winning coalition by implementing policies which favor one's supporters at the expense of one's opponents. Even if an elected official is morally opposed to such a base use of political power, he or she has little choice. After all, potential opponents are formulating their own platforms which will not hesitate to offer rewards from the use of political power in order to attract a winning coalition. The politicians are aided and abetted in this process by the lobbying of special interest groups, which attempt to elicit favorable government programs in return for future campaign support, particularly in the form of financial contributions.

The role of the bureaucrats likewise comes under scrutiny by the public choice theorist. As noted above, bureaucrats are also assumed to be motivated by individual self-interest, which is often translated as a desire to maximize the size of the bureaucracy (either in terms of personnel, budget, or both) which the bureaucrat controls. As a result, bureaucratic size and activity continually increase, going beyond the efficient level of provision of government services. Because the government is a monopoly, there are no competitive checks on this process of inefficient expansion.

To the public choice theorist, then, the world of democratic politics is considerably nastier than that envisaged by the classical theory of democracy (and implicitly by the neoclassical normative theorist.) Is it possible, however, that from this process there will emerge a set of policies which promote the common good? It does not appear promising. Some analysts conclude that because of extensive logrolling by elected officials to further the interest of their own constituencies, the size of the government will be too big.[7] Others argue that this tendency is more than offset by a neglect of public goods, which often result in relatively small benefits to any one individual and thus are not as useful in attracting votes. The end result of these tendencies is a government which is too small.[8] Whatever the outcome of this debate, it is clear that the government has become in the eyes of the positive public choice theorist a tool for promoting narrow self-interested legislation rather than programs for the common good.

How does a capitalist economic system fit into this framework? Because the economic situation of an individual is one of the (if not *the*) most important determinants of individual utility, the institutional arrangement of a particular economic system will be crucially important in determining the parameters of self-interest around which special interest groups form. In a capitalist economic system, the owners of the means of production would presumably form one interest group. (On other issues, individual capitalists may be members of other special interest groups which actually oppose one another). As such, they would be in competition with other interest groups for control of political power. How successful this group is in controlling government is not theoretically determinate, being a function of relative political skill (such as lobbying and propagandizing the public) vis-à-vis other interest groups. It might be expected that the capitalist group has some inherent advantage, given their generally greater financial resources. But greater financial clout alone presumably cannot always guarantee victory, and the capitalist class will find itself constantly jockeying with other interest groups for control of the government. The theory itself does not yield a prediction of the ultimate fate of this particular group.

We would be remiss if we did not note the intellectual similarities between Schumpeter and the public choice theorist in their analysis of the workings of the democratic political system. Both are unsympathetic to the classical theory of democracy and its emphasis on the "common good" and the "will of the people." Both see the democratic process as a competitive struggle for the control of political power. Both analyze the actions of political actors from a self-interested perspective. Both see the struggle for political leadership as a battle to win control of the government in order to use the government to promote one's own interests. Schumpeter was clearly a forerunner of the current field of positive public choice, a point little noted by the profession.[9]

D. The Marxian Analysis

In the capitalist system, Marxists assert, workers lose control over their own lives: they only find work when the capitalist finds it profitable. Thus human needs may go unmet, factories may lay idle with workers seeking employment, but unless capitalists see a profit-making opportunity, the market mechanism is not set in motion. This lack of coordination and cooperation is seen as fundamentally irrational by Marxists.

Irrational or not, the system is maintained because those who have economic power ascend to positions of political power or are able to exert their power over those who do. Marxists thus scoff at the idea of the capitalist system being the main support of democracy. If it is a democracy, they claim, it is a perverted one—primarily for the rich and powerful. From their positions and through their connections, capitalists are able to use the state to further their own ends. They set up the educational system, thereby transmitting capitalist ideology to the country's youth. They set up the courts and appoint the judges, thereby assuring the sanction of private property. They run the newspapers, radio stations, magazines, and television stations. The notion of the efficacy and equity of the capitalist system permeates the entire social system, argue the Marxists, through this subtle but pervasive system of propaganda.

The state is seen by Marxists as a manifestation of concentrated economic power. To deny that the rich and the corporations they control possess vast power is folly; the point is to discover how they wield it through the political system. First and foremost, the state protects private property, that is, the interests of the capitalist class. As the Marxist theorist Ralph Miliband put it, "the state in these class societies is primarily and inevitably the guardian and protector of the economic interests which are dominant in them. Its *real* purpose and mission is to ensure their continued predominance, not to prevent it."[10]

Thus we have seen that Marxists view the state as essentially the mistress of the capitalist class. Now we must turn to their view of the specific favors the mistress performs. We utilize James O'Connor's analysis of the state,[11] recognizing that there is substantial disagreement among Marxists regarding the specifics of state behavior.

O'Connor begins with the premise that the state must fulfill two functions: accumulation and legitimization. The former, an offensive function, is to provide "social capital." Of this function there are two subcategories: "social investment," i.e., infrastructure which increases the productivity of labor; and "social consumption," i.e., disability insurance which lowers the wage capitalists must pay workers. The legitimization function, a defensive one, is to delude the workers into believing the system is equitable and, thus, to quell social unrest. Included are "social expenses" covering items like food stamps, Medicare, and Medicaid. They must be extracted by government out of business profits, though according to Marxists the state only provides these services to maintain a conducive atmosphere for the capitalists. These two functions—accumulation and legitimization—are the dual and contradictory goals of the capitalist state, and the consequence of attempting to fulfill both is economic, political, and social crisis. The crisis arises because the state must grow (through the accumulation process) to maintain and increase monopoly capital; but as a result of the ensuing growth of monopoly, there is increased unemployment, inflation, stagflation, and poverty, calling for an even larger state (through the legitimization process). In other words, as O'Connor states, "the growth of the state is both a cause and effect of the expansion of monopoly capital."[12] The ever-increasing growth of the state translates into ever-increasing expenditures for legitimization and accumulation, but the profits these expenditures generate are entirely appropriated by monopoly capital. The ensuing crisis is a result of the growing demands upon the state's shrinking purse.

The only practical solution to the fiscal and social crisis

which will enable capitalism as a system to survive is for the state to cooperate more fully with monopoly capital to encourage production (that is, lower costs) in both the state and private sectors. In other words, the answer is a social-industrial complex (SIC) which will retain profits in the private sphere while relieving the fiscal pressure. For the SIC to emerge, three political changes are required. First, the "ties between monopoly capital and the state will have to become even closer." Second, "the influence of competitive capital, particularly its influence and power in local and state government and in Congress, would have to be weakened." And, third, "stronger bonds between monopoly capital and organized labor would be necessary."[13]

O'Connor and other Marxists do not gladly greet the emerging SIC. They envision it as redistributing income from labor to the owners of capital through taxation by the state. In other words, all taxpayers will fund the activities of the SIC, but the benefits will accrue to capitalists.

Marxists, like neoclassicals, see an intimate relation between the political apparatus that governs society and the economic sector which guides production. There, obviously, the similarity ends. Neoclassicals view capitalism as a liberating economic system transmitting its noncoercive basis to the polity. Marxists believe the oppressive nature of the capitalist system is pervasive in the structure of the state. In effect, the state is seen as the dictatorship of the ruling class over the remainder of society.

Only when productive property has been transferred from the private to the public sector has real democracy a chance to develop and flourish. At that time the "owning" class will be the vast majority—the workers—and its representative—the state—will serve that class.

E. Institutionalist Approach

Institutionalists believe that in limiting economics to a study of maximizing behavior, traditional economists engage in a level of theoretical abstraction that is too high and a scope too narrow to deal adequately with current social problems, let alone understand the complicated world around us. Specifically, the most glaring examples are illustrated by mainstream theorists ignoring, or relegating to unimportance, the crucial issues of technological change and the exercise of power in the economy and the polity. Matters such as these are of vital importance in explaining inflation, unemployment, stagflation, inadequate health care and housing, corporate flight, rural and urban poverty, to mention a few of the major problems facing our society today.

In addition, several areas of contention exist between neoclassicals on the one side and institutionalists on the other which will serve to highlight the different roles of the state each favors. Traditional economists maintain that society is simply a collection of individuals, while institutionalists see society as an organic whole greater than the sum of its individual parts. In addition, their views vary greatly on the nature of human behavior. Whereas mainstream economists believe human behavior is fundamentally rationalist, atomistic, and hedonistic, institutionalists conceive of a broader human nature which allows a place for habit, custom, sense of adventure, even perversity, in addition to acquisitiveness. Institutionalists also utilize a broader conception of the economic system. Specifically, whereas neoclassical economists downplay the existence or importance of power in the hands of any individual economic agent, institutionalists place at the center of their analysis an explicit consideration of certain powerful institutions: large corporations, unions, the state. Finally, while institutionalists value freedom no less than neoclassicals, they contend that in some ways the market system restricts rather than promotes freedom. Basic freedom requires adequate food, shelter, health care, and education, which, institutionalists assert, the private market system seldom provides for all. Thus, intervention by the state is frequently necessary to make freedom real for the poor.

Institutionalists see the growth of government as a natural phenomenon required to re-embed the economy into the social system. They argue that a study of history shows that the free-market economy in the sense of a self-regulating system is a utopian vision. Individual markets have always existed (at least for commodities), but an economy run by free markets required the actions of government to come into existence. The mercantilist controls over the economy that laissez-faire economics fought against were merely that era's way of embedding the economy into the social system. The attempt to "free" markets (particularly for labor, land, and capital) from societal control was a failure. No one was willing to live with the results of a pure market system. No one, in practice, would accept the notion that everything and everyone's worth was measured by a market-determined price. Workers formed trade unions to eliminate competition in the labor market, business firms merged or sought government regulation to eliminate competition. Farmers sought government price supports. Consumers sought government protection from the free market in the form of pure food and drug acts, and on and on. Professionals convinced government that the public welfare demanded the licensing of lawyers and physicians.

Thus, if anything is "natural" it is the social control of the economy as a way of embedding it in the total social system; and, if anything is "unnatural" it is a laissez-faire system of self-regulating markets. It is not only government that interferes with our private lives but even more so an unregulated market system. Therefore, institutionalists argue that the burden of proof should lie with the free-market devotees. History and common sense make the real issue "what type of policies should we use to obtain the economic results we want without allowing the economy to dictate our social and political values and needs."

As a result of the need to oversee this re-embedding process government has become a primary economic agent along with business firms, labor unions, and consumers.

Consequently, institutionalists argue that any relevant economic theory must provide a central role for government as an *actor*, not just a referee or umpire. This leads institutionalists to become advocates of national economic planning. They see the private economy becoming ever more dominated by large firms with a consequent decline in the disciplinary power of competition. Attempts to restore competition fly in the face of the historical evolution of society. Both efficiency and freedom require that the visible hand of the national income accountant supplement the invisible hand of competition in directing the U.S. political economy.

IV. VIEWS OF THE WRITERS EXPRESSED IN THIS VOLUME

With this background of Schumpeter's views and the general framework of contemporary thought from which the writers in this volume emerge, we are now prepared to turn specifically to their writings. In this section we wish only to give a brief description of their major themes, leaving to the reader the experience of more fully exploring their analysis. We begin with the article by Warren Samuels, which most directly addresses Schumpeter's analysis. It is followed by Gary Becker's neoclassical positivist approach, then by Samuels Bowles's Marxian-oriented exposition.

A. Warren Samuels, the Institutionalist

As an economist steeped in the institutionalist school of economic thought, Warren Samuels cannot help but be impressed with the breadth of Schumpeter's analysis of the functioning of the economic system. The conception of an economic system as an evolutionary phenomenon, the importance of socio-cultural interactions with the economy, the attention devoted to the effect of the economic system on the political process and vice-versa, and the crucial role of class are all issues which the institutionalist school consider vital in understanding the workings of an economic system. But admiration does not necessarily mean agreement, and Samuels offers a reinterpretation of Schumpeter's analysis with dramatically different conclusions.

The first part of Samuels's paper reviews the major themes developed by Schumpeter. One theme which Samuels emphasizes is the role of government in Schumpeter's analysis. He notes with approval that Schumpeter clearly recognized the essential nature of politics, which is the competitive struggle for control of the government in order to use it to promote one's own interest. However, he criticized Schumpeter for having "failed consistently to recognize or make explicit deeply and thoroughly enough that in capitalist society dominance is institutionalized by capitalist control of government, that government functions to institutionalize and cement the capitalist system and capitalist dominance." While Schumpeter certainly recognized that the bourgeois class uses the democratic system of government to establish the capitalist order, Samuels argues that he refused to take this basic insight to its logical conclusion. This shows up most clearly in Schumpeter's private-public dichotomy. Schumpeter implies that the private sphere relates to those activities which are governed by private contract, while the public sphere implies activities governed by the "democratic method, that is to say the sphere of politics." In the opinion of Samuels, this distinction is not meaningful, given Schumpeter's own analysis of the role of government. The issue is not so much the dividing line between private and public activities, but rather whose interests are being served by the government when this line is drawn. In Samuels's words,

> What is nominally private is so because of certain public arrangements and policies. What is nominally public is profoundly influenced by the structure of private economic and political power. The dividing line between private and public in commercial society, and the very notion of government *interference*, is reflective not of legal-economic reality but of the bourgeois world view.

Or, "stated differently, the issue is not . . . the economic function of the state but the group for whom the state functions." This basic argument of Samuels provides the motivating rationale for the other Schumpeterian themes which he discusses in section I, those of hierarchical social structures, the process of leadership selection, discipline of the labor force, and the use of political power.

In section II of this article Samuels turns his attention to Schumpeter's analysis of the evolution of capitalism, in particular to the conclusion that capitalism will not survive, but rather is destined to be replaced by socialism. Samuels begins his critique with an examination of Schumpeter's definition of capitalism and socialism. At first blush Schumpeter appears to define capitalism in the traditional manner—that is, as an institutional arrangement characterized by private ownership of the means of production and the regulation of the production process by private contract. But, Samuels asks, does not this narrow economically based definition of capitalism violate the very essence of Schumpeter's analysis, namely, the concept of capitalism as not just an economic arrangement but an entire ordering of society determined by the values and interests of the entrepreneurial or bourgeois class? The very brilliance of the Schumpeterian argument lies in his understanding that capitalism means a capitalist *society,* not a particular economic arrangement operating within whatever cultural environment it may find itself. The two are inextricably linked. Samuels posits the following definition of capitalism as actually used analytically by Schumpeter.

> Capitalism . . . is a system of order, or rule, in the interests of the capitalists (or entrepreneurs or bourgeoisie) as those interests are defined by their definition of reality and their value system. More specifically, capitalism is the system and the world of the individualist entrepreneur, and its demise the demise of the individualist entrepreneur and his class.

In this last phrase we have the crux of Samuels's understanding of Schumpeter's analysis and the basis of his disagreement with Schumpeter's conclusion on the future of capitalism. When Schumpeter says that capitalism cannot survive, what he really means is that the dominant position in society of the individual entrepreneur, and the bourgeois class which relied on this group, cannot survive. This group will no longer be able to control the power of the state to protect and further its interest, that is, to define the public-private dichotomy in a manner which solidifies its position in the social hierarchy. What Schumpeter has traced out, brilliantly and admirably, is the gradual erosion of a social system dominated and defined by the interest of a bourgeois class reliant on the skills of the individual entrepreneur. Understood as such, Samuels would agree that the analysis has been largely proved correct by the tide of events since Schumpeter's prediction.

Agreement does not exist, however, on the crucial issue of what will replace the system of individual entrepreneurial capitalism. Schumpeter, of course, argued that socialism was the heir apparent. But what did he mean by the term *socialism*? In "The March into Socialism" Schumpeter states:

> I define (centralist) socialism as that organization of society in which the means of production are controlled, and the decisions on how and what to produce and on who is to get what, are made by public authority instead of by privately-owned, privately-managed firms. All that we mean by the March into Socialism is, therefore, the migration of people's economic affairs from the private into the public sphere.[14]

The key elements here (and elsewhere when Schumpeter defines socialism) are central authority and public rather than private control.

There are some problems here, according to Samuels. Recalling that, properly understood, capitalism to Schumpeter meant individual entrepreneur capitalism, where does the corporate form of capitalism fit into the capitalism-socialism dichotomy? With its concentration of ownership of the means of production and run by a managerial elite commanding a bureaucracy of highly trained specialists, it evidences elements of socialism. But it is privately owned and thus has elements of capitalism. Is this "private socialism" or "public capitalism"? Schumpeter himself is ambiguous, as demonstrated by his argument concerning the "socialization" of the souls of businessmen by "big business capitalism."

> What I am suggesting, then, is that *by Schumpeter's own account*, individualist entrepreneurial capitalism and public-sector control of production and distribution are not the only alternatives. By his own account, the corporate system seems to be a third alternative. . . .

But this definitional difficulty in classifying the modern corporate form of business organization reflects a more basic flaw in Schumpeter's definition of socialism. For the definition ultimately rests on a public-private distinction, and, as we noted above, Samuels does not find this a meaningful distinction in light of Schumpeter's own analysis. For it was Schumpeter who taught us that democratic politics was a struggle for control of the political process in order to use the state to further one's own interest. Whenever we see the phrase "public control," therefore, are we not compelled by Schumpeter himself to ask the question "For whose interest?" And if the answer to this question is "the interests of private business," do we not have capitalism in its essence? The class of people who define this interest may have changed, but it is still a class which through the control of government and other social institutions shapes and defines society for the protection and furtherance of private business interests.

This is the argument which Samuels puts forward for our consideration. Stripped to its essentials, what Schumpeter has described to us is not the change of an economic system, but rather the change in the nature of the ruling class of the economy. In Samuels's words, "Schumpeter's argument ultimately involves a change in the leadership strata of the economy and society. . . . [He] focuses on what may be perceived as a new and different leadership stratum *within capitalist society*; different and new in that it is the corporate administrator succeeding the individualist entrepreneur, but still nominally capitalist." (emphasis added). Viewed from another perspective, Schumpeter has presented some convincing arguments concerning why the dominant role of the individual entrepreneur will erode and disintegrate. He has not made a convincing argument concerning why the emerging dominance of the corporate manager will likewise disintegrate.

The conclusion flowing from Samuels's analysis is straightforward. "Capitalism is not dying. . . . As it turned out, Schumpeter traced the development of the corporate system, the passing, not of capitalism, but of the old individualist entrepreneurial stage or form of capitalism." Can this new system of corporate capitalism survive? We cannot tell. It will depend on how well this new form of capitalism can produce a leadership stratum which is capable of protecting and promoting its interests through the control of government and other social institutions. We have Schumpeter to thank for pointing out to us the fundamental importance of this factor.

B. Gary Becker, the Neoclassical Positivist

Gary Becker's paper does not directly address the question of the survival of capitalism or the interaction of democracy and capitalism. Rather, it develops a model of the behavior of political pressure groups that indicates which types of groups are likely to acquire substantial political power. The model, Becker claims, is general enough to be applied to various types of political systems, all of which (even dictatorships) will be characterized by groups which attempt to bend government policies in their favor. The type of political system will be crucial in defining certain variables in the model, but this does not detract from the generality of the analysis.

Before Becker begins the formal presentation of his model,

he does direct a few brief comments explicitly towards Schumpeter's arguments in *Capitalism, Socialism, and Democracy*. He is critical of Schumpeter's belief that a socialist economic system could result in less political activity by self-interested pressure groups. For workers, in particular, Schumpeter argued that a socialist system might command more moral allegiance than a capitalist system, since a socialist government would be promoting the interests of workers (at least, theoretically). This would presumably result in less political pressure by workers to influence the government. Becker notes that this argument is disappointingly naive, especially in light of the actual experience of socialist societies (which he defines to include the Soviet Union and China). "Contrary to Schumpeter, I believe that selfish pressure groups . . . have an incentive to be more rather than less [politically] active under socialism . . . because a much larger fraction of resources is controlled by the state under socialism than under capitalism."

Despite this disagreement, the thrust of Becker's paper is to provide a formal model for understanding certain characteristics of the competition for political influence. As such, it is clearly within the Schumpeterian spirit of viewing the political process—democracy, in particular—as a competitive struggle for political leadership. He begins with the standard neoclassical utility-maximizing assumption, in this case applied to political pressure groups. That is, political pressure groups are assumed to attempt to maximize the well-being of their members. He begins by assuming two such groups exist, with identical incomes before government redistribution. After the government redistribution, the subsidized group will have higher incomes and the taxed group will have lower incomes. The monetary amounts of these transfers must be equal. But a key point in Becker's analysis is that these revenue flows will not, in general, represent either the full cost on the taxed group or the net benefit to the subsidized group. On the taxation side, the amount of revenue collected will be less than the full cost imposed on the taxed group if there are any efficiency losses (in economists' language, "deadweight losses") resulting from the imposition of the tax. The losses may occur, for example, if the imposition of a tax results in disincentives to invest or work. A subsidy may also create efficiency losses, with the result being that the monetary amount of the subsidy overstates the net gain to the subsidized group. Thus, while revenue flows are equal between the groups, the total cost of the tax will exceed the total gain from the subsidy as a result of efficiency losses from the transfer. (Except in the presumably rare case of nondistorting taxes and subsidies.)

Becker then introduces into his model what he calls "influence functions," which will determine the amount of taxes paid (negative influence) or subsidies received (positive influence). For example, the amount of monetary subsidy a group receives will equal the amount of positive political influence the group exerts. This influence will depend positively on the amount of political pressure the group applies, negatively on the amount of political pressure applied by the opposing (taxed) group, and whatever other variables are relevant, such as age, occupation, etc. A similar function exists for the taxed group, and its (negative) influence will equal the amount of taxes paid. Because the amount of the tax equals the amount of the subsidy, the two influences are equal with opposite signs. In other words, the amount of subsidy received will equal the positive political influence of the subsidized group, which also equals the negative political influence of the taxed group. As such, then, political influence is a zero-sum game in terms of revenues and subsidies in that an increase in influence by one group exactly equals the decrease in influence by the other group. Furthermore, political influence is a negative-sum game if efficiency losses increase the real cost of taxation or reduce the value of a subsidy.

Becker completes his model with the addition of a political pressure production function, which determines how much political pressure a group exerts. This, as noted above, is a key variable in determining how much influence the group exerts. Becker postulates that the amount of pressure exerted will depend on two variables, the number of members in the group and the amount of resources (time, money, etc.) which are devoted to producing pressure. This latter variable, in turn, will equal the amount of resources spent per member multiplied by the number of members. He notes two factors of particular importance with regard to this function. One is economies of scale (with regard to expenditure of resources) in producing pressure. At low levels of expenditures, adding additional members to the group can be expected to have a positive payoff in terms of political pressure, for their addition to expenditures will enable economies of scale to be realized. As more and more members are added, however, this effect will be diminished. On the other hand, adding more members can be expected to increase the probability of free riding on the group, and this will offset to a degree any advantages to be gained from economies of scale.

With the model specified in this manner, equilibrium conditions for the market in political pressure can be derived. One property of the model which is particularly significant concerns the response by one group to an increase in the political pressure applied by another group. In general, the pressure exerted by one group will increase when the pressure by an opposing group is raised, primarily as a result of the increasing deadweight losses as taxes and subsidies are increased. The implication of this is that there are inherent checks on the amount of favors a particular interest group can extract from other groups via the use of state power. As one group attempts to gain additional subsidies through increased political pressure, opposing groups will be motivated to increase their pressure on the government in order to prevent a lowering of their income.

Becker next discusses four specific propositions which flow from his analysis of the market for political pressure.

One obvious implication of the above model is that a group which becomes more efficient at producing political pressure will be able to reduce its taxes or raise its subsidy. However, this is a relative effect, in the sense that the group must become relatively more efficient in producing pressure as compared to an opposite group. In a zero-sum game, the relative strengths of the two groups is the crucial variable.

Becker is particularly concerned with the role deadweight costs play in the market for political pressure. It will be recalled that deadweight costs drive a wedge between the tax revenue collected and the total cost of the tax on the taxed group, and between the amount of subsidy paid and the net benefit from subsidy. If deadweight costs exist, then the total cost of the taxed group will necessarily be larger than the net benefit to the subsidized group. Because of this, an increase in deadweight costs will reduce the equilibrium subsidy. The extreme example best illustrates this proposition. If raising one dollar of tax revenue imposes substantially higher costs (say $100) on the taxed group, the benefit from increased pressure to prevent this taxation will be augmented, thus resulting in more pressure. On the other hand, if the one dollar of revenue to be raised results in a considerably lower net benefit (say ten cents) to the subsidized group as a result of inefficiencies, there is less incentive for the subsidized group to exert pressure. This proposition implies that there exists some "tyranny of the status quo" in that deadweight inefficiencies give an intrinsic advantage to the taxed group vis-à-vis the subsidized group, *ceteris paribus*. This intrinsic disadvantage can be overcome with greater efficiency in producing influence. From this proposition Becker notes that "the importance of the private status quo does not imply that politicians are lackeys of the rich and is even consistent with the poor being more successful politically." Maintaining the status quo, however, is not necessarily synonomous with a laissez-faire role of the government, for it may require government activity to maintain the status quo against shocks and fluctuations in the private economy.

An interesting corollary to this proposition is that policies which raise efficiency are more likely to be adopted than policies that lower efficiency. Becker demonstrates that policies which increase aggregate efficiency—that is, which correct for market failures, such as the existence of pure public goods and externalities—give an intrinsic advantage to subsidized groups, and thus are more likely to be undertaken. With this corollary Becker is able to bridge the gap between his positive theory and the neoclassical normative theory of the public expenditures.

A final proposition derived from Becker's model is that the competition among political pressure groups favors efficient methods of taxation. Holding tax revenue constant, a more efficient form of taxation will impose less of a burden on the taxed group and thus will be favored by them. The reduction in burden also reduces the amount of political pressure exerted by the taxed group, and, *ceteris paribus*, will increase the subsidy to the subsidized group, even as the net income of the taxed group is increased.

C. Samuel Bowles, the Marxist

Samuel Bowles is concerned about power in a democratic capitalist system and in particular the accountability of power. Politics, in his view, is a practice whose object is to wield power so as to transform or stabilize the rules or institutions which shape and constrain people. The purpose of his paper is to demonstrate that liberal democratic theory, which maintains that in a capitalistic society the state secures the accountability of power, is flawed beyond repair. A democratically elected government cannot guarantee an accountability of power in a capitalist society. Only abolition of the capitalist mode of production can ensure this result.

Bowles begins his critique by outlining the development of the liberal democratic theory of the state. The theory was developed to answer what Bowles calls "the Grand Question of Liberal Theory: how is it possible to develop a set of institutions which will allow for the rational coordination of the social division of labor and which are at the same time compatible with a nonabsolutist state." The idea was to develop a system which would promote economic progress while simultaneously guaranteeing individual freedom. The answer, of course, was liberal democratic capitalism. A private (i.e., capitalist) market economy would promote economic growth while maintaining freedom in private affairs by ensuring that any constraints on individual freedom would be either a result of natural factors (e.g., genetically determined) or else would be voluntarily self-imposed as a result of entering into contracts. With regard to constraints imposed by the state, the democratic political system assured that such contraints would be held accountable to the views of the majority of the citizens. People would engage in political activity in order to influence the state to promote their own interests, but any action by the state would (at least implicitly) reflect the desires of the majority of the people.

This theory, which in essence is the neoclassical normative theory of the state and the economy, represents what Bowles calls the state conception of politics. This view holds that politics (the setting of constraints, i.e., rules, other than those imposed naturally or voluntarily) occurs only with respect to state activity. There are two major components to this view: the contractual nature of civil society, and the instrumental view of political practices. Bowles attacks both of these components in order to discredit the state conception of politics, which lies at the heart of liberal democratic theory.

The contractual nature of civil society is that part of the theory which maintains that constraints (other than natural constraints) imposed on the individual outside the political sphere are voluntary, self-imposed constraints flowing out of freely made contractual relations. In Bowles's view, this is not an accurate representation of relations in a capitalist society. He focuses in particular on the wage labor contract, the predominant method of labor relations in a capitalist system. When an employer and employee enter into a wage labor contract, the worker agrees to exchange his time in return for a pecuniary reward. But the employer is not concerned with the worker's time per se (it can't be marketed as an output) but rather the product which can be produced with that time (in combination with capital). But how the worker's time is converted into output of goods and services is not part of the wage labor contract (this is to be compared with a labor service contract, in which a particular amount of output, or service, is negotiated for in exchange for payment). In Marxian terms, this is the problem of extracting labor from labor power. The rules which govern the relationship cannot be characterized as either contractual or electoral, in the sense that they are accountable to some democratic process. Rather, other social factors (such as the owners' desire to maintain a hierarchical production process, the motivation of workers, etc.) determine the nature of this relationship. Whatever the factors may be, the result is that this aspect of civil society—an aspect which imposes constraints on individuals—is not governed by contractual relations.

In addition to this, Bowles argues that the actual production of labor power (human capital, in neoclassical terms) is likewise not governed by contractual relations. The education and attitudes a person acquires is a function of the family and the educational environment in which the person is raised. To argue that this process can be characterized as determined by contractual arrangements voluntarily entered into by the individual is clearly inappropriate.

Thus Bowles concludes that at least two major aspects of civil society—the capitalist-labor relationship and the production of labor power—cannot be represented as resulting from voluntary contractual agreements. Both these aspects are governed by a set of rules or institutions which impose constraints on the individual. Hence they represent power, and thus are political, but are not accountable to a democratic electoral process. To this Bowles added a third argument to support the contention that civil society is not governed by voluntary contractual arrangements or democratically accountable procedures. The standard neoclassical model assumes a given set of preferences, technological possibilities, and distribution of property. The distribution of property is determined by the state, which he assumes for the sake of argument is democratically accountable. From these initial conditions, an individual's income constraint will be determined by the combination of initial ownership of physical and human capital and the price structure determined by the private competitive market system. The problem, argues Bowles, is that there is not a unique price structure arising out of these initial conditions, as has been demonstrated by the British side of the Cambridge Capital Controversy.[15] If this is true, what determines which set of possible prices is actually realized, which will in turn determine the individual income constraint? Bowles argues that it is unreasonable to assume that the actual outcome is determined solely by the state (which would make the resultant income constraint democratically accountable), but rather it represents the interaction of the state and other social factors which are not accountable. In sum, then:

> We may thus conclude that the noncontractual relations in civil society exert not only direct personal limiting effects on their participants, but indirect limits via their likely role in the determination of the structure of prices as well.

Having thus disposed of the contractual nature of the civil society component of the liberal democratic state conception of politics in a capitalist society, Bowles turns his attention to the other major component of that theory—the instrumental view of political practices. The instrumental view argues that political practices are intended to mobilize resources in order to use the state to advance one's interests. He labels this "the politics of getting." The basic shortcoming of this approach of political activity is that it assumes that interests (preferences) are exogenously determined. In other words, preferences are determined separately from the political activity itself. In fact, no consideration of how preferences are formed is given in this view, which results in an inadequate characterization of political practices. In Bowles's view, the very act of political activity will shape preferences—that is, people engage in activities which alter their preferences. This he calls the "politics of becoming." But there are socially imposed constraints on this process of preference transformation or, more fundamentally, on the process of human development. The education of the individual would be one such constraint. The question becomes that of deciding what determines these socially imposed constraints. This question is crucial, for if it can be demonstrated that preference-shaping constraints are determined in an accountable manner (for example, that they are set by the state), then the instrumental view of politics would be restored and justified as a component of the liberal democratic theory. Stated differently, the assumption that the preferences (interests) which motivate political activity are exogenously determined would still be consistent with the liberal democratic theory if it were understood that the assumption implied that these preferences arose from a set of social constraints determined by a democratically accountable system. If, on the other hand, the socially imposed constraints on preference determination can be shown to stem from nonaccountable sources, then the entire accountability of power justification of the liberal democratic theory is called into question.

And this is precisely the result of Bowles's analysis. He bases his conclusion on two basic propositions. The first is that the domain over which the electoral state extends does not include two crucial preference-shaping institutions: the family and the capitalist-worker relationship. Of course, in liberal democratic theory the state is not meant to exert authority over these relationships, as they are in the domain of the contractual civil society. But, as already demonstrated, neither the family nor the capitalist wage labor mode of production can be adequately characterized as contractual. Since both of these institutions shape preferences, but both are neither contractual nor state controlled, they consequently both represent socially imposed constraints on preferences which are neither voluntary nor democratically accountable.

Can it not be argued, however, that the state has *potential* control over these institutions, and that the default in extending this control stems from a democratically determined decision, thus implicitly making these institutions accountable to majority consent? Bowles rejects this line of reasoning. He poses the question somewhat differently. In a capitalist society, does the electorate really have a choice to alter the capitalist production process? Bowles doesn't think so. For one, the threat of a "capital strike" (the refusal of capitalists to invest unless a "good" investment climate is maintained), with its resultant unemployment and recession, will effectively prevent elected officials who are concerned about their re-election possibilities from going against the wishes of the owners of capital. And by preventing the social experimentation necessary to demonstrate to the electorate that an alternative system can work, the capitalist can effectively inhibit any groundswell of popular opinion for a radical break from capitalism.

But even if the domain of the state were extended to cover the capitalist production process and family, the liberal democratic capitalist system would still limit the accountability of social structure to majority will. This is because liberal democratic capitalism does not produce a "democratic culture"—an environment which encourages the practice of democratic methods. Democracy is no different from anything else in that it takes practice to operate skillfully and effectively. Practice at democratic, collective decision making is not encouraged by the liberal democratic competitive capitalist system. First of all, the hierarchical nature of the capitalist production process is inherently antidemocratic. Secondly, competitive markets themselves discourage democratic practices. The decision to engage in democratic practices will be a function, among other things, of the opportunity cost of not engaging in such practices. Competitive markets, by offering alternatives to the results to be acquired through democratic practices, lower the opportunity cost of not participating in democratic practices. An example Bowles uses is the school system. If your child is attending public school and you are unhappy about some aspect of it, one alternative is to attempt to organize other parents and voice your discontent to school officials. This would be practicing democracy. However, if a competitive market for schools exists and there is a private school option open to you, you might elect that option rather than engage in democratic practice. Finally, the liberal democratic emphasis on individual rights and freedom does not encourage collective choice based on solidarity and cooperation. For these reasons, then, the liberal democratic capitalist system is not conducive to promoting practices which will result in the effective expression of the majority will.

In the end, then, the liberal democratic conception of the capitalist system results in the existence of significant amounts of social power, accompanied by socially imposed constraints on individuals, which are unaccountable.

> We conclude that the unaccountable determination of the decision to invest, the structure of the labor process, markets, and liberal democratic discourse itself render both the determination of social constraints on choice and the development of wants effectively unaccountable in the liberal democratic capitalist model.

Is there an alternative? Bowles admits that to date a better answer to the Grand Question has yet to be developed. He notes that Marxist theories of the state and politics are subject to criticisms similar to those made against the liberal democratic theory. In conclusion, Bowles offers his own views toward the direction political economy theorists must go in order to develop a truly democratic, egalitarian social system.

IV. A COMPARISON OF THE DIFFERENT APPROACHES

As the reader will soon realize, the writers presented in this book approach the problem of analyzing the relationship between politics and economics from radically different perspectives. We comment briefly in this section on some of the fundamental differences in their approaches, differences which reflect basic disagreements among contemporary schools of thought in this area of political economy.

Gary Becker's analysis is paradoxically the most general and the most narrow. It is general in the sense that his model, with the proper specifications, can be applied to any political system. In particular, a specification of his political influence function would differ across systems and would be crucial in determining who actually wields political power in any given society. In certain respects, Samuels and Bowles have indicated in their analyses some of the factors which they would consider important in specifying these functions in a capitalist democracy. But it is the assumption Becker makes to narrow his inquiry which most sharply distinguishes him from the other writers. Most important, he assumes an initial public-private dividing line (which is unspecified) from which the competing parties begin their struggle to alter. He also assumes a set of fixed preferences which motivate the actors in his model. From these initial conditions he derives a set of static equilibrium conditions, along with some comparative static properties of the model. The approach is firmly within the mainstream of neoclassical microeconomic analysis.

Warren Samuels's institutionalist approach would not necessarily reject the Becker analysis of the issue, but rather would extend the scope of inquiry into the assumptions underlying the Becker model. In particular, Samuels would probably feel compelled to examine the initial public-private dividing line which Becker assumes. He might make the following observation. Take two groups, A and B, with initial income Ya and Yb. After government redistribution, the incomes of the two groups are Y′a and Y′b. If Y′a is less than Ya, Becker labels the difference a "tax" on A resulting from government action. Likewise, if Y′b is greater than Yb, the difference is labeled a "subsidy" to B resulting from government action. But, Samuels would ask, is it not equally accurate to label the difference between Ya and Y′a a "subsidy" to A resulting from the government action which established the initial equilibrium condition? This government action may consist of the enforcement of private rights and nothing else, but this is government action all the same. Whether one labels the change in A's income a tax or a subsidy will reflect one's ideological preference with regard to the establishment of the initial rules under which the game is to be played. To put the argument more concretely, let's call group A the "capitalist" and group B "the workers." If we start with the distribution of income which would occur under a government-enforced capitalist economy and examine the changes which result from a movement by the government to a socialist economy, the decrease in the capitalists' income would be labeled a tax in the Becker model. But a socialist would counter that the appropriate way to analyze this change is to begin with the distribution of income which would exist in a socialist economy, and determine the change which occurs when the state decides to establish a capitalist economy. Under this assumption, the higher income of the capitalist in a capitalist economy would represent a subsidy to the capitalist. Samuels would merely note that both are correct. Whether the change is labeled a tax or a subsidy depends on the initial assumptions, the appropriateness of which will depend on the ideological values of the individual.

Because the initial assumptions in the Becker model are arbitrary, it can be applied to either an initially capitalist economy or socialist economy. This reflects the generality of the model. Thus Samuels's approach does not represent a criticism of the Becker approach, but is more in the nature of a warning to potential users regarding proper application and interpretation of the model. However, we suspect that Samuels would be critical of some of the conclusions Becker draws from his model. Becker chastises Schumpeter for his naivety in believing that political competition might be less in a socialist society than in a capitalist society. Becker believes that political activity would be greater in a socialist society "because a much larger fraction of resources is controlled by the state under socialism. . . . " We think Samuels would disagree with this statement—not with the conclusion, with which he might agree—but with the reasoning supporting the conclusion. Even in a strict laissez-faire capitalist economy, the state controls resources via its enforcement of private property rights and the contracts extending from them. In other words, the state still draws and enforces the public-private dividing line. Considerable political activity can be generated by attempts to change this line, or to change the system which establishes these rules of the game. From Samuels's institutionalist perspective, the state always determines the distribution and allocation of all society's resources by its establishment of the rules of the game, which will favor some groups at the expense of others. Interest groups will fight to change the rules—to alter the public-private dividing line[16]—no matter whether the system is laissez-faire capitalism or state socialism. Whether one system generates more political activity than another will be a function of the controlling group's ability to solidify their position (through ideological indoctrination,[17] superior economic performances, etc.) rather than where the public-private line is drawn, as Becker indicates.

Becker also concludes from his analysis that "the importance of the private status quo does not imply that politicians are lackeys of the rich, and is even consistent with the poor being more successful politically." The "tyranny of the status quo," it will be recalled, results from the existence of deadweight losses in taxing and subsidizing, which lower the benefits from a subsidy and increase the cost of the taxation.

Samuels would probably be troubled by this statement. One problem is the use of the adjective *private* to describe the initial distribution of income. As noted above, the assumed initial distribution can represent a wide range of government activity in establishing that distribution—to label it "private" could be quite misleading. More important is the conclusion reached, which is revealing in ways which Becker probably did not intend. Becker's definition of being "successful politically" means being better organized, better funded, etc. Becker is saying that the poor can be better organized politically and still not be able to change the initial distribution of income, a testimony to the importance of the political power and success of the group which set the original rules of the game.

While Samuels extends Becker's concept of politics to encompass the determination of the initial distribution of income, Samuel Bowles goes further. Politics to Bowles is "a practice whose object is the transformation or stabilization of those rules (forms of organization and discourse) which define the family, the state and capitalist production." The establishment of the rules which govern any institution in society is a matter of politics, not just those rules which determine the structure of government. Rules are intended to shape and constrain individuals and as such are political, no matter the arena in which the contest is played. Consequently, in analyzing the interrelationship of a particular economic-political system, one should look not only at effects on the actions of the state, but also at the effects on the other institutions which influence what type of person an individual will become. In the same spirit, Bowles also explicitly rejects the Becker model in its assumption that individuals' preferences are given, that is, are determined exogenously to the system. In Bowles's view, a key aspect of politics is the shaping of individual preferences, which will be a function of the institutional rules by which people live. To ignore this would result in a failure to understand the "vibrant social movements which have already left their mark on the twentieth century."

Thus we see considerable differences in the approaches these authors take in analyzing the relationship between the economic and political spheres. Not surprisingly, these differences stem primarily from different perceptions concerning the problem to be addressed. The Becker model is aimed primarily at explaining the consequences of political activity as it occurs today (or, more correctly, as it has occurred in the recent past and can be expected to occur in the near future). Hence he takes the existing institutional arrangements of society as given and derives propositions theoretically about the likely consequences of political activity undertaken within that framework. Thus Becker can make some interesting observations concerning why government might be expected to bail out Chrysler Corporation. Samuels and Bowles are much more concerned about how the existing institutional arrangements came to be established and how they might evolve in the future. As such, they take a more dynamic, historical perspective (one more in the spirit of Schumpeter, it might be noted). Their approach is aimed more at explaining, for example, why the United States moved from a laissez-faire system in the late nineteenth century to the welfare capitalism of today, rather than why the government decided on the Chrysler bailout. Consequently, one's opinion concerning the usefulness of the different approaches will be a function of the particular problem which one is addressing.

VI. CAPITALISM, DEMOCRACY AND SCHUMPETER TODAY

One test of the intellectual greatness of an individual scholar is whether his arguments become over time a generally accepted model with which to analyze a particular set of problems. We conclude this introductory overview with an assessment of how Schumpeter's analysis has stood this test of time. Do the thoughts expressed by the writers in this volume represent an extension of Schumpeter's line of reasoning, or has the force of his arguments withered over time?

With respect to the nature of a democratic political system, the views expressed in this book seem to be firmly in the Schumpeterian spirit. Little trace of the classical theory of democracy can be found. Democratic politics has been transformed from a search for the "common good" as expressed by "the will of the people" into a competition for political control in order to use the power of the state to protect and promote one's own interest. This is clearly the thrust of the analyses advanced by all of the current writers. There does appear to be some disagreement concerning whether this competitive struggle will result in at least the partial attainment of the common good, a point mentioned by Schumpeter via an analogy to a competitive struggle for profits. From Samuels's institutionalist perspective, such a conclusion is hopelessly laden with value judgments concerning what constitutes the common good. If one's values are such that one believes that the interests which the democratic state is currently promoting are the interests which it should be promoting, then one might naturally conclude that democracy has attained the common good. If not, then the democratic process would be seen to be promoting the narrow self-interest of politically powerful groups. Becker's analysis is similar, although more optimistic. While recognizing that narrow self-interest will be the motivating force behind democratic politics, his model indicates that policies which raise aggregate efficiency (i.e., are Pareto efficient) have an intrinsic advantage in favor of adoption. Under the assumption that Pareto efficient policies promote the common good, Becker's analysis indicates that the common good at least will not be totally neglected. However, the fact remains that democratic governments will be under constant pressure to promote the interests of politically powerful groups. But, according to Becker, this will be true of *all* governments, not just democratic governments. The advantage of democracy is that it allows for the free development of opposing political pressure groups, which act as a check on the influence any one group can exert on the government. Thus, democracy is seen by Becker as a way of minimizing the harm which could result from the inevitable attempts of pressure groups to use the government to promote their narrow self-interest.

Bowles has a different perspective on the relationship of the democratic system and the common good. He puts a good deal of faith in the democratic process, so much so that it is as if the process is what really counts. If a truly democratic system—defined as a free and informed competitive struggle for the votes of the people—were operative, then good results would follow automatically. True democracy means that the individual has a voice in determining all the institutional rules. Utilizing that voice in the establishment of the institutional rules of society which all must share is part of the process of becoming a fully developed human being. To Bowles, democracy promotes the common good because participation in the democratic process is itself part of the common good.

In any event, the basic Schumpeterian thesis that democracy represents the competitive struggle for political leadership appears firmly entrenched. There also seems to be general agreement with the Schumpeterian argument that the success (or lack thereof) of the capitalist class in controlling the democratic process will be crucial to the survival of capitalism. Considerable disagreement exists, however, concerning how well the capitalist class will fulfill this task. Schumpeter believed that as the nature of the capitalist economic system changed, the capitalist class could not survive politically, in the sense that they would not be effective in protecting their class interest from competing groups in the democratic struggle. Samuels, the only writer who explicitly addresses Schumpeter's analysis on this issue, simply rejects his conclusion. While Schumpeter accurately foresaw the decline of the role of the individual entrepreneurial class and its eventual replacement by the corporate managerial class, he did not convincingly demonstrate that this new capitalist class would inevitably lose the competitive struggle for control of the reins of government. Although continued control of that class is not guaranteed, it will certainly be a powerful force in the democratic battle. Bowles implicitly recognizes the potential staying power of capitalism when he admits that to date no better answer to the Grand Question of Liberal Theory has been advanced. Becker's model indicates that the status quo has an intrinsic advantage, a result consistent with the prediction that the entrenched capitalist class will be difficult to dislodge. In sum, none of these authors are willing to join Schumpeter in writing the obituary for the capitalist system.

In the final analysis, however, whether present-day scholars agree or disagree with the specific conclusions of Joseph Schumpeter is not of crucial importance, for his basic themes continue to have intellectual vitality. Forty years after the publication of *Capitalism, Socialism, and Democracy*, the issues raised are still of fundamental concern, and the arguments advanced still evoke thoughtful consideration. This book is proof of that.

NOTES

1. We will be quoting from the third edition (New York: Harper & Brothers, 1950).

2. Or, more correctly, democracy will not necessarily be replaced as capitalism is replaced.

3. Pareto efficiency is defined as an allocation of resources such that no reallocation can increase the utility of any one person without decreasing the utility of some other person in the economy.

4. The reader may argue that the growth goal does not enjoy universal acceptance, as witnessed by the environmentalists' criticism of the ecological damage rendered by the growth of the industrial society. We wish to sidestep these criticisms by defining growth as a general increase in the well-being of the population, a defini-

tion which would require an accounting of any environmental costs resulting from increased output of goods and services.

5. Kenneth J. Arrow, *Social Choice and Individual Values* (New York: John Wiley & Sons, 1951, rev. ed. 1963).

6. Anthony Downs, *An Economic Theory of Democracy* (New York: Harper and Row, 1957).

7. Gordon Tullock, "Some Problems of Majority Voting," *Journal of Political Economy*, December, 1959.

8. Anthony Downs, "In Defense of Majority Voting," *Journal of Political Economy*, April 1961.

9. This statement is based primarily on the observation of Dennis Mueller. See his *Public Choice* (Cambridge: Cambridge University Press, 1979), p.1, n.1.

10. Ralph Miliband, *The State in Capitalist Society* (New York: Basic Books, 1969), p. 265.

11. James O'Connor, *The Fiscal Crisis of the State* (New York: St. Martin's Press, 1973).

12. Ibid., p. 29.

13. Dwayne Ward, *Toward a Critical Political Economics* (Santa Monica: Goodyear Publishing, 1977), p. 213.

14. In *Capitalism, Socialism, and Democracy*, 3rd ed., p. 413.

15. The Cambridge Capital Controversy centers precisely on the question of the uniqueness of the competitively determined price structure, in particular the uniqueness of the price of capital. The debate acquires its name from the fact that the leading protagonists are located in Cambridge, Massachusetts (Harvard University and the Massachusetts Institute of Technology) and Cambridge University in England. The American side is identified with the view that there is a unique set of prices (at least under reasonable assumptions concerning the production relationship), while the British side is identified with the view that in general there is not a unique set of competitively determined prices.

16. In Schumpeter's terms, the devotion of resources to this struggle represents "the wastes that result from the conflict of structural principles in a social body" (*Capitalism, Socialism, and Democracy*, p. 198).

17. This would appear to be what Schumpeter had in mind when he argued that a socialist system might result in less political competition because the workers would feel more "moral allegiance" to a social government.

A Critique of Capitalism, Socialism, and Democracy*

Warren J. Samuels

Joseph Schumpeter was one of the awesome giants of economics and, indeed, the social sciences during the first half of this century. Remarkable in the range and depth of his intellect, raised in the upper echelons of Viennese society, Schumpeter did not hesitate to interpret and judge his discipline and his civilization. *Capitalism, Socialism, and Democracy* is one of the truly profound analytical and interpretive works of the twentieth century.[1] It is one of the few books in economics—are there more than a dozen?—with which every aspiring economist must come to grips. Most of Schumpeter's other books were of the first rank, but few rival the relentless and comprehensive interpretive power of this one.[2]

I shall confine my attention to *Capitalism, Socialism, and Democracy,* specifically the third American edition of 1950, which includes chapter 28, written in 1946, on the consequences of World War II; the preface to the third English edition of 1949; and the somewhat incomplete written version of "The March into Socialism," Schumpeter's 1949 Presidential Address to the American Economic Association. These additions to the original work of 1942 indicate that Schumpeter did not materially alter his interpretation during his final years.

My purpose is to re-evaluate the argument of *Capitalism, Socialism, and Democracy.* In section I, I shall identify certain deep, important, and perennial topics dealt with in the book. Due to the importance of Schumpeter's well-known central argument, these topics are readily neglected, their importance eclipsed by the argument itself. They are very important, however, as preliminaries for the critique and interpretation of the argument I shall render in section II. I also, to some extent, shall critique his treatment of those topics as a prelude to section II, which examines the central argument of the book. That argument is very powerful but, I believe, subtly flawed because of an important hiatus in his argument. I contend that the argument may not be what it appears to be and offer a different interpretation, largely on Schumpeter's own ground.[3] Throughout the discussion I shall treat his argument both in its own terms and in relation to my perception of reality.

My principal argument is that, on Schumpeter's own terms, what succeeds (individualist entrepreneurial) capitalism is not historic socialism but corporate capitalism. The latter may be seen as another stage of capitalism or as private socialism but more readily comports with Schumpeter's understanding of capitalism culturally considered. I also argue that Schumpeter's analysis involves neither capitalism versus socialism nor private versus public but a transformation of the leadership strata of (capitalist) economy and society. In making those arguments, I am not quibbling over what Schumpeter *intended* but offering a reinterpretation on his own terms of what I believe his analysis amounts to.

Several preliminary considerations are in order.

First, *Capitalism, Socialism, and Democracy*, indeed, Schumpeter's work as a whole, is not easily interpreted. His analysis has great breadth, depth, complexity, and subtlety. It comprises both ideology and science, both positive and normative elements, which are not readily distinguished. His concepts and definitions, most notably of capitalism, socialism, and government, have a somewhat kaleidoscopic quality. His work can be approached from a number of quite different perspectives and be interpreted differently.[4] His analysis at the level of fundamentals is so penetrating, subtle, and delicate as to render uncomfortable, if not suspicious, those accustomed to more confined social inquiry. Some are made uncomfortable and suspicious by his evident biases.

Schumpeter is universally, and correctly, perceived as elitist if not aristocratic. He also has been designated as both right wing and conservative,[5] and "socialist," "old-time socialist," "neo-Marxist," "old neo-Marxist socialist," and "a veteran of the international socialist movement since 1905,"[6] terms not to be taken at face value.

Schumpeter himself insisted that his was a purely positive analysis, limiting himself largely to footnote indications of where his personal preferences differed from his analysis.[7] He distinguished the moral aspects of developments from economic arguments.[8] He distinguished identification of facts and of the tendencies indicated by facts from both prediction-prophecy and desirability.[9] He disclaimed both advocacy and prediction[10] as well as defeatism (which he says has meaning only in reference to action and not to analysis).[11]

As for myself, I shall endeavor to let Schumpeter's ideas speak for themselves without characterization (although with reinterpretation). I shall try to be positive, not normative, in interpreting and assessing his ideas; that is, I shall be necessarily subjective but shall withhold any intended judgment as to the desirability of either the fruition of his perceived trends, if they were to be realized, or actual developments with which his analysis is to be compared. For example, Schumpeter stressed social structure—hierarchy—as the key to understanding systemic operation, performance, and evolution. He also largely adopted, normatively, the perspective of the individualist entrepreneurial elite. I shall agree with him regarding the importance of social structure as a positive matter but shall refrain from adopting the perspective of any social class and from either applauding or denigrating any hierarchical system. I also shall not attempt to interpret either Schumpeter's motives, as some have been wont to do, or his putative effect on policy and reality.

I. MAJOR CHARACTERISTICS AND THEMES

A. Characteristics

Schumpeter's was one of the great architectonic minds in economics in the twentieth century. He was a synthesizer on the grand scale: notice his integration of the business cycle work of Clement Juglar, Joseph Kitchin, and N. D. Kondratieff. More than that, Schumpeter was able to conceptualize and theorize in original ways about the economic system as a whole at the level of the deepest elements of political economy and of systemic evolution. He could focus on the political economy and also, more narrowly, on the market per se. In both areas his analysis was penetrating. Technique did not obscure conceptual fundamentals: notice his treatment of prices as coefficients of choice rather than as representative or constitutive of an independent, deterministic category.

No less than the institutionalists, whose work Schumpeter did not appreciate, Schumpeter was holistic and evolutionary. Although not articulated in Darwinian or Veblenian terms, his evolutionism encompassed the profound ideas of systemic change, creative destruction, and the economy as a disequilibrium process. Cumulative causation also is present in his work. His holism meant that economics was more than the study of market resource allocation. Economics to Schumpeter was political economy. Economics encompassed what he called "economic sociology." The economy encompassed the market plus legal-institutional and social-structure arrangements. No less than did John R. Commons he dealt with the organization and control of the economic system *qua* system. Political economy (or economic sociology) deals with power, social structure, leadership, leadership selection, and social discipline. The multifaceted problem of order, most especially the conflict between hierarchical and egalitarian forces, is everywhere evident in his work. Schumpeter did not take systemic parameters and symbolization (or myths) fully for granted, notwithstanding his own blinders and selective perception.

This last point is important: Candor, perhaps to the extent of demythification if not demystification, was a significant characteristic of Schumpeter's work, being not the least impressive in *Capitalism, Socialism, and Democracy*. Candor, of course, is a matter of perspective. What is a candid recognition, or admission, to one reader may be myopia, if not bias, to another; and a statement deemed candid nonetheless may be wrong.[12] Be that as it may, Schumpeter treated extensively and candidly topics which other writers have tended to shun, perhaps because of perceived threats to ideology, policy, and system. As we shall see, these are among the major themes supportive of the central argument of the book: the importance of social class and social structure for interpretation of economic affairs; the socio-economic role of leadership and leadership selection; control and discipline of the human labor force; the centrality of power; democracy as competition for political leadership rather than constitutive of the common good and the general will; and certain legal-economic fundamentals. What I consider Schumpeter's candor may be due to such factors as the great depth of his analytical penetration on both sides of issues and the great subtlety of his own performance of the high priest role. It seems also to be attributable to his profound consciousness that socioeconomic arrangements were the result of human action, choice, and policy, that natural laws and verities (however useful their articulation may be in mass manipulation) did not of themselves dictate the course of social evolution.

Schumpeter's candor need not be discussed solely on such an abstract level. Whether we deem his views right or wrong, he candidly acknowledged certain sensitive points: The test of efficiency neglects distributional and structural considerations and is therefore limited.[13] The principle that competition maximizes output requires assumptions reducing the proposition to little more than a truism.[14] Capitalist evolution is unable to eliminate the evils of poverty and unemployment.[15] Although adequate provision for the unemployed may impair the conditions of further economic development,[16] control of inflation may achieve little but increased difficulties for business.[17] No merely economic argument for or against socialism can be decisive.[18] Some of the sweeping indictments of capitalism have a qualified justification.[19] Under capitalism the nature of economic phenomena is masked by the profit interest.[20] Competition largely is a myth.[21] Individualism and socialism are not necessarily opposites.[22] Bureaucratization of economic life has proceeded very far.[23] Propositions concerning the working of democracy are meaningless without reference to times, places, and situations.[24] Socialism would not require a change in human nature.[25] Socialism is possible and could work, however regrettably,[26] but "Before humanity chokes (or basks) in the dungeon (or paradise) of socialism it may well burn up in the horrors (or glories) of imperialist wars."[27]

There are other examples as well: The views of the classical economists were those typical of "the English bourgeois class, and bourgeois blinkers are in evidence on almost every page the classical authors wrote." Still, they may have been "speaking the truth."[28] Indeed, "there was, if anything, less of absolute nonsense in the old harmonistic view—full of nonsense though that was too—than in the Marxian construction of the impassable gulf between tool owners and tool users."[29] Although even conservatives are seen to borrow from the arsenal of the demagogue,[30] "nursery tales are no monopoly of bourgeois economics."[31] If the masses are deemed unable to compare alternatives rationally, all economic actors, far from evidencing solely voluntary choice, have their behavior and choice constrained and conditioned by forces which shape their choosing mentalities and narrow the list of possibilities from which they can choose:[32] The capitalist process "reshapes not only our methods of attaining our ends but also these ultimate ends themselves."[33] Addressing himself to questions of moral allegiance, incentives, and responsibility,[34] Schumpeter acknowledged that "socialist management may conceivably prove as superior to big-business capitalism as big-business capitalism has proved to be to the kind of competitive capitalism of which the English industry of a hundred years ago was the prototype. It is quite possible that future generations will look upon arguments about the inferiority of the socialist plan as we look upon Adam Smith's arguments about joint-stock companies which, also, were not simply false."[35] Although fighting for socialism must be coupled with a perception of what kind of socialism will work, it is neither nonsense nor wickedness to fight for socialism.[36] Moreover, there is no necessary relation between socialism and democracy (as he defines these terms), certainly no incompatibility,[37] and, contrary to an early form of the Hayek-Mises argument, rational and determinate production decisions can be reached under socialism.[38]

There is considerable irony in such candor: Schumpeter is eminently rationalist here, no less than the "intellectuals" so frequently castigated by him. He certainly recognized the need for a system of faith[39]—a system of faith presuppositions which legitimizes a status quo—but no small amount of the argument in the book amounts to a critique and demythification of some of the leading rationalizations of status quo Western economic and political arrangements. If, as Schumpeter argued, capitalist processes rationalize ideas, chasing metaphysical and romantic beliefs from our minds,[40] then Schumpeter himself clearly was a child of capitalism.[41]

B. Themes

However one interprets Schumpeter's candor, *Capitalism, Socialism, and Democracy* treats—typically directly, explicitly, and without apology—certain important, deep, and perennial topics not often prominent in works by economists, topics readily eclipsed by Schumpeter's argument itself but necessary for its full if not proper interpretation. These topics, with their related substantive themes, largely constitute Schumpeter's deep, broad, realistic political economy, or economic sociology. Two of these topics are Schumpeter's legal-economic realism and a related emphasis on the ultimate competition comprising a contest for the control of government.

1. *Government*

Although he does not go as far as I would prefer, one has to be impressed with Schumpeter's depth of understanding of the interrelationships between legal and economic processes. Although Schumpeter was personally attracted by the idea of a limited state and insisted on the reality of the distinction between private and public spheres (to which I shall return), the book as a whole comprises an exercise in political economy, not economics. It stresses both the inseparability of economy and politics, that is, the reality of a legal-economic nexus, and the effective recognition of same by both the political-economic right and left. Government is involved quite intimately in what in another connection Schumpeter calls "all that really matters—in the principles governing the formation of incomes, the selection of industrial leaders, the allocation of initiative and responsibility, the definition of success and failure"[42]—in the entire physiognomy of the economy. Not only are "*some*" legal and moral restrictions implicit in the very nature of an economic system,[43] but also government is the protective frame of the bourgeois system.[44] Moreover, economic and political activity are alternative, substitutive modes of seeking advantage:

> we see in the process why and how class action, always remaining intrinsically the same, assumes the form of political or of business action according to circumstances that determine nothing but tactical methods and phraseology.[45]

Politics and economics are not different spheres: They are different arenas of action; the choice is a matter of tactics.

Schumpeter admired Marx's effort at integrating politics and economics:

> Wars, revolutions, legislation of all types, changes in the structure of governments, in short all the things that non-Marxian economics treats simply as external disturbances do find their places side by side with, say, investment in machinery or bargains with labor—everything is covered by a single explanatory schema.[46]

It was the singleness of the Marxian explanatory schema to which Schumpeter objected: "There is indeed a grand wedding of political facts and of economic theorems; but they are wedded by force and neither of them can breathe."[47] In Schumpeter's view, politics and economics interacted. There are political, social, and economic causes and implications[48] of all the phenomena of the political economy. Marx improved upon economics by showing the hidden political meanings behind technical answers to technical questions. But while politics no longer is "an independent factor that may and must be abstracted from in an investigation of fundamentals and, when it does intrude" be treated as a "naughty boy" or *deus ex machina*, politics is made by Marx "determined by the structure and state of the economic process and becomes a conductor of effects as completely within the range of economic theory as any purchase or sale."[49] To Schumpeter, rather, as I read him, economic structure and performance are fundamentally influenced by politics, and politics by economic behavior and choices as well as performance.

Schumpeter is manifestly bourgeois in holding that private productive activity is sensitive to government action,[50] that government action is incompatible with the efficient working of the private enterprise system,[51] and that social reform and the struggle for social legislation can impair the conditions of further economic development.[52] The state, indeed, is not generally able to take the "longer view."[53] But Schumpeter is much more complex than that: Government is the necessary protective frame of the bourgeois system.[54] There is "certainly an element of truth in" the *Communist Manifesto*'s teaching that "the executive of the modern State [is] . . . a committee for managing the common affairs of the whole bourgeoisie."[55] For all its tribulations, "The middle class is still a political power."[56] "Rational as distinguished from vindictive regulation by public authority turns out to be an extremely delicate problem. . . ."[57] There is some justification for expanded government enterprise.[58] Political structure is influenced by the structure of private economic power.[59] The social function of parliment is to produce legislation.[60] And so on.

Schumpeter clearly recognized that government in a bourgeois society is essentially a bourgeois phenomenon.[61] His theory of democracy rejects the ideas of common good and popular will and substitutes a competitive struggle for votes: Democracy, to Schumpeter, involves a competition for political leadership, the exercise of electoral choice of leaders in political competition.[62] But it seems to me of the utmost importance that Schumpeter's conception of democracy as a competition for political leadership be seen to involve ultimately and fundamentally a continuing contest for the control and use of government itself—vis-à-vis laissez faire and other minimalist myths which function to obscure the fundamental role of government in the capitalist (indeed, any) economic system. The crux of politics includes capturing office *and* the capture of government in order to make and change the law to enhance the situation and opportunities of one group or another. The contest is over the terms on which each group, or class, puts the state to its own use and advantage. "Bourgeois legality" signifies for Schumpeter both the negative view of the state and the affirmative bourgeois use of the state: The so-called parsimonious state is the vital obverse of a legal system used to effectuate the bourgeois view of the world, to "guarantee bourgeois legality."[63]

The rise of the capitalist bourgeoisie and of the national state had been, after all, related processes.[64]

Schumpeter felt that the bourgeoisie were unable to rule, that they required the protection of a hierarchical social structure and of a government run by a historical ruling aristocracy.[65] Whatever one thinks of this view, clearly Schumpeter envisioned a symbiosis between the bourgeoisie and aristocracy to use government for the protection of the class interests of the upper strata[66] and of the interests of society defined by the upper strata. Not once but twice does he observe "that the capitalist order entrusts the long-run interests of society to the upper strata of the bourgeoisie."[67] Government is thus the object and vehicle of control by the propertied, and they are the propertied in part because of their control of government.

One can identify or not with the bourgeoisie and/or aristocracy in this matter. But Schumpeter's treatment in this book of the struggle to control the state—notwithstanding his essentially rationalist effort to compare and contrast the prospects of capitalism, socialism, and democracy—is analytically straightforward. It clearly echoes his 1918 essay on the crisis of the tax state, in which he observed:

> The kind and level of taxes are determined by the social structure, but once taxes exist they become a handle, as it were, which social powers can grip in order to change this structure.[68]

Here we have the center of the legal-economic nexus clearly penetrated. Moreover:

> it is, however, decisive for a realistic understanding of the phenomen [*sic*] of the state to recognize the importance of that group of persons in whom it assumes social form, and of those factors which gain dominion over it. [Here Schumpeter appended a note which includes the following: "It is always important to recognize who or whose interest it is that sets the machine of the state in motion and speaks through it. Such a view must be repulsive to anyone for whom the state is the highest good of the people, the acme of its achievement, the

sum of its ideas and forces. However, only this view is realistic. It also contains that which is correct in the otherwise wrong theory that the state is nothing but the ruling classes' means of exploitation. Neither the aspect of a class state nor the idea of the state as something above all parties and classes which is simply the organized 'totality,' is adequate to the nature of the state. Yet neither of the two is taken out of thin air. The state does always reflect the social power relations even though it is not merely their reflection. The state does necessitate the emergence of an idea of the state to which the peoples give more or less content depending on circumstances, even if it is not the offspring of an abstract idea of the state embracing the social whole."] This explains the state's real power and the way in which it is used and developed.[69]

Nonetheless, Schumpeter may have failed consistently to recognize or make explicit deeply and thoroughly enough that in capitalist society dominance is institutionalized by capitalist control of government, that government functions to institutionalize and cement the capitalist system and capitalist dominance—which is to say that Schumpeter did not fully succeed in transcending his own bourgeois perspective. This is perhaps most clear in his treatment of the private-public dichotomy.

The basic point I want to make is that Schumpeter's use of the distinction between private and public does not give full effect to his own deep analysis of legal-economic reality, in part because of his own bourgeois perspective. But let me first review his uses of the dichotomy. The principal use not unexpectedly involves his definitions of commercial and socialist societies. A commercial society "is defined by an institutional pattern of which we need only mention two elements: private property in means of production and regulation of the productive process by private contract (or management or initiative)." Although he often speaks of capitalism and bourgeois society and economy, he focuses definitionally on commercial society, one which "is not as a rule purely bourgeois. . . . Nor is commercial society identical with capitalist society. The latter, a special case of the former, is defined by the additional phenomenon of credit creation. . . ." But commercial society, "as an alternative to socialism, in practice always appears in the particular form of capitalism," and Schumpeter himself largely keeps to "the traditional contrast between capitalism and socialism."[70] So the alternative to socialism is private economic activity, private economic control through private contract or management.

Socialism is "an institutional pattern in which the control over means of production and over production itself is vested with a central authority—or, as we may say, in which, as a matter of principle, the economic affairs of society belong to the public and not to the private sphere."[71] Accordingly, by the "March into Socialism" Schumpeter means "the migration of people's economic affairs from the private into the public sphere."[72] Schumpeter goes out of his way to avoid the term "state ownership" and insists that he does not use it in his definition of socialism[73]—wherein he contemplates a Central Board or Ministry of Production which is neither exclusive nor absolute.[74] The state, he says, "should not be allowed to intrude into discussions of either feudal or socialist society, neither of which did or would display that dividing line between the private and public spheres from which the better part of its meaning flows."[75]

Some thirty pages later Schumpeter goes on to say that the "outstanding feature of commercial society is the division between the private and the public sphere—or, if you prefer, the fact that in commercial society there is a private sphere which contains so much more than either feudal or socialist society allocates to it. This private sphere is distinct from the public sphere not only conceptually but also actually," he says. "The two are to a great extent manned by different people . . . and organized as well as run on different and often conflicting principles, productive of different and often incompatible standards." He then speaks of the "wars of conquest waged upon the bourgeois domain with ever-increasing success by the men of the public sphere." "Most activities of the state in the economic field then appear in the light that is well characterized by the old bourgeois economist's phrase, government *interference*."[76] The state, after all, through taxation "has been living on a revenue which was being produced in the private sphere for private purpose and had to be deflected from these purposes by political force."[77] Socialism, then, involves the extension of "the democratic method, that is to say the sphere of 'politics,' to all economic affairs"[78] — an interesting formulation which, when juxtaposed to earlier conceptions, equates economic with private and politics with public.

One could quibble with Schumpeter about definitional tautologies, definitional ambiguities, and the nature of and/or nomenclature appropriate to the formal governing apparatus of a socialist society as he uses the term throughout the book. Such questions may involve more than quibbles: Schumpeter certainly is unclear as to the relationship between (1) economic control in the private versus public spheres and (2) private versus public ownership, and especially whether (or when) *public* is a synonym for *state*. I raise at this point a different but related matter: Is the distinction between private and public very meaningful in light of Schumpeter's own, other analysis? I think not. I think that the dichotomy is swamped by his more general analysis. At the deepest levels of analysis — not, that is to say, at the level of the ideologue — commercial, capitalist, or bourgeois economy and society are what they are because of bourgeois (or bourgeois-aristocratic) dominance of the state. Private property is what it is, in most if not all particulars, because the state protects certain interests as property and not others. What is nominally private is so because of certain public arrangements and policies. What is nominally public is profoundly influenced by the structure of private economic and political power. The dividing line between private and public in commercial society, and the very notion of government *interference*, is reflective not of legal-economic reality but of the bourgeois world view. Granted, there often is antagonism between the personnel of the state and certain special bourgeois interests,[79] and the scope of effective nominally private discretion is in some immediate sense greater under capitalism than under socialism. Nonetheless, at the deepest levels of analysis (that is, without system symbolization) the distinction breaks down. By Schumpeter's own analysis capitalism (or whatever one wants to call it) exists because of the imposition of bourgeois legality on the state and the enforcement of bourgeois legality by the state upon all social powers, among other things toward preventing the consolidation of social interests in a manner deemed antagonistic to capitalist society and interests.

Stated differently but to the same effect, the issue is not, or not so much, the economic function of the state but the group for whom the state functions; the issue is not "interference" by the state but for whom and to whose advantage.

I shall have more to say about Schumpeter's distinction between capitalism and socialism, and the meaningfulness of his central argument, in section II. At this point I applaud his frequent attention to what I consider to be legal-economic fundamentals, including his theory of democracy as a competition for political leadership (to which I also shall return) and what I consider its most significant derivative, the notion of competition for the control of government itself. But I fault his use of the private-public distinction in a manner which strongly tends not to give full effect to those legal-economic fundamentals, including the significance of political competition. This mixture of realism and bias, of his insight and blinders, is suggested by Schumpeter's insistence that distribution is only in socialism, and not in capitalism, a distinctly political matter (see note 12). The mixture also is suggested by his argument that the socialist blueprint will be superior, in part, due to the elimination of waste in resources hitherto dedicated to the struggle over the control of government economic policy which transpires in capitalism.[80] But cannot one expect resources to be devoted to influencing economic policy under socialism—especially if distribution is recognized as distinctly political? Indeed, by Schumpeter's own analysis of bureaucratization—the decision-making apparatus of large, highly organized, and populous units—one can expect considerable use of resources in decision making per se. But here we come to another aspect of Schumpeter: his belief in the making of technical solutions by experts, consideration of which I also defer to section II.

2. *Social Structure: Hierarchism and Leadership Selection*

A further theme pervading *Capitalism, Socialism, and Democracy,* indeed, one which is fundamental to his argument and to my interpretation of that argument, centers on Schumpeter's belief in and acceptance of the reality of hierarchic leadership structures in both particular institutions and society itself. His description of Frank William Taussing may be applied quite accurately to Schumpeter himself: "He was among those few economists who realize that the method by which a society chooses its leaders in what, for its particular structure, is the fundamental social function . . . is one of the most important things about a society, most important for its performance as well as for its fate."[81]

There are several strands in Schumpeter's emphasis on hierarchic social structure. One of them is *class.* Interestingly, it would appear that the class facet of Schumpeter's analysis largely has been filtered out of subsequent discussions of the book. His argument is stated largely in terms of the demise of capitalism through its success, with generally only passing reference made to capitalists as a group and especially as a "class." Explicit public consideration of class is now largely beyond polite discussion in economics (and in the larger world), and articulation of Schumpeter's argument specifically in terms of class would constitute acknowledgement of the relevance of class. In a world in which life, power play, and the use of government continue unabated, whatever the perceived ultimate fate of capitalism, recognized classism would be both unseemly and unsafe.

But Schumpeter's analysis is developed, not merely couched, in terms of class; he continually speaks of the capitalist class.[82] It is, after all, "the capitalist class's economic position [that] is bound to crumble in time."[83] His concept of class is not rigid; the incessant rise and fall of families into and out of the upper strata is to him the salient point of social classes, aside from their existence.[84] Capitalism has embodied a new class comparable, more or less, to the old ruling class.[85] The bourgeoisie comprise "the leading class,"[86] "the upper strata of capitalist society."[87] There is "capitalist art," "the capitalist style of life," and "classwise rights."[88] The entrepreneurs form part of the bourgeois class and perform its social function.[89] "Economists," Schumpeter complained, "have been strangely slow in recognizing the phenomenon of social classes."

> Social classes . . . are not the creatures of the classifying observer but live entities that exist as such. And their existence entails consequences that are entirely missed by a schema which looks upon society as if it were an amorphous assemblage of individuals or families. It is fairly open to question precisely how important the phenomenon of social classes is for research in the field of purely economic theory. That it is very important for many practical applications and for all the broader aspects of the social process in general is beyond doubt.[90]

A second strand is *leadership*. Schumpeter can say that the long-run interests of society are entrusted to the upper strata of bourgeois society[91] because, in his view, therein lies the social leadership which organizes production, engages in saving and investment, and controls and disciplines the human labor force of society.[92] The role of hierarchy in society is, broadly speaking, to provide social leadership.

A third strand is *leadership selection*: "The same apparatus which conditions for performance the individuals and families that at any given time form the bourgeois class, *ipso facto* also selects the individuals and families that are to rise into that class or to drop out of it."[93] The role of leadership selection is critical to Schumpeter. Indeed, the crumbling of the capitalist class's economic position is due in part to the failure of that class to reproduce or replenish itself with viable leadership material.[94]

A fourth strand is Schumpeter's view that those who rise to and remain in the upper, elite strata of society are superior individuals. The bourgeois "is a class which, by virtue of the selective process of which it is the result, harbors human material of supernormal quality. . . . "[95] The upper strata have superior intelligence, talent, and energy—in short, they are supernormal-quality human material.[96]

It is, of course, not irrelevant to argue that determinations of superiority are, or at least tend to be, system- if not class-specific. Systemic and leadership performance need not be undertaken solely on a system's or leadership group's own, self-glorifying and self-serving, terms. Schumpeter, of course, was chagrined at the perceived accumulating weakness of bourgeois leadership and extrapolated from it and other factors the self-destruction and decomposition of the capitalist system.[97] Vilfredo Pareto, in contrast, felt that if a ruling class failed, then it deserved to fail; and Friedrich von Wieser, Schumpeter's early mentor, stressed the historical transformation of leadership in society.

There are several aspects of Schumpeter's hierarchism which I shall deal with below. The principal one has to do with Schumpeter's apparent central argument. In my view, the argument only superficially involves the passing of capitalism and the rise of socialism. More fundamentally, in Schumpeterian terms, it involves a transformation of the leadership strata. The juxtaposition of capitalism and socialism, which is admittedly Schumpeter's, only obscures the critical role of hierarchical structure and change of leadership. Closely related thereto are, first, Schumpeter's quiet emphasis on the critical nature of the control and discipline of the human labor force, and, second, his strong belief that economic management by social leadership, however constituted, must be insulated from interference by politicians and politics, especially democratic politics in either a capitalist or socialist system. With the exception of the question of labor discipline, these matters are addressed in section II.

3. *Discipline*

A further important theme pervading *Capitalism, Socialism, and Democracy* is a concern with discipline, a perceived need in every economic system to control and discipline the human labor force. Schumpeter, I think, would have been receptive to Bertrand de Jouvenel's observation that "Whoever does not wish to render history incomprehensible by departmentalizing it—political, economic, social—would perhaps take the view that it is in essence a battle of dominant wills, fighting in every way they can for the material which is common to everything they construct: the human labor force."[98] Schumpeter would have agreed and gone further to emphasize the necessity of disciplining the human labor force by those in control, whatever the economic system.

As regards discipline, he says:

> there is an obvious relation between the efficiency of the economic engine and the authority over employees which, by means of the institutions of private property and "free" contracting, commercial society vests with the bourgeois employer. This is not simply a privilege conferred upon Haves in order to enable them to exploit Have-nots. Behind the private interest immediately concerned there is the social interest in the smooth running of the productive apparatus.[99]

He distinguishes "authoritarian discipline, which is taken to mean the habit, inculcated by agents other than the disciplined individuals themselves, of obeying orders and of accepting supervision and criticism" from self-discipline, which—"in part, at least . . . is due to previous, even ancestral, exposure to the disciplining influence of authority" and also group discipline "which is the result of the pressure of group opinion on every member of the group and similarly due, in part, to authoritarian training undergone in the past."[100]

This analysis, to repeat, applies to all economic systems

but is introduced as a prelude to a discussion of the comparative advantage of discipline in a socialist system. He argues that socialist society will not be able to dispense with authoritarian discipline although it will be less necessary than in a society of fettered capitalism, and authoritative enforcement of discipline will prove an easier task in socialism. Schumpeter stresses that "we need not project the tendencies inherent . . . very far ahead in order to visualize situations in which *socialism might be the only means of restoring social discipline*" (emphasis in original). He concludes, "it is clear in any case that the advantages which a socialist management will command in this respect are so considerable as to weigh heavily in the balance of productive efficiencies"[101] – because of the greater force of dismissal, less constraint on the use of authoritarian discipline, greater motivation to uphold authority, no government opposition, and the greater centrality of economic necessities.[102]

It should be clear that whatever the positive and normative merits of these complex matters, Schumpeter obviously places himself in the position of the employer, what I would call the universal manager point of view. Labor is not to make its own unencumbered and unchanneled choice between work (=real income, or goods) and leisure. Schumpeter's analysis provides only superficially for the aggregation of individual worker preference, such as they are. More deeply, it posits disciplined preference and motivation, with the discipline undertaken and targeted by the managers, perhaps formerly capitalist managers, afterward socialist managers. "After all, effective management of the socialist economy means," says Schumpeter, "dictatorship not *of* but *over* the proletariat in the factory,"[103] a situation not, in his view, very different from that in capitalism. Elsewhere, Schumpeter laments that the increased permissiveness of bourgeois society limits the role of discipline.[104] Only Russia has solved the problem of industrial discipline.[105] One advantage of socialist or quasi-socialist parties in Europe after World War II was that "they were the very people to administer the right dose of social reform, to carry it on the one hand, and to make the masses accept it on the other."[106] Schumpeter does not generally think highly of those whom he considers politicians, but he does state that "there is one very important thing" that the politician "knows professionally, viz., the handling of men."[107]

4. *Power*

Finally, I must note that as a work in political economy the common thread running through Schumpeter's legal-economic realism (however mixed) and his emphases on competition for the control of government, on classism and social structure, on leadership and leadership selection, and on control and discipline of the human labor force, is *power*. Schumpeter *is* concerned, in his comparison of the capitalist and socialist blueprints (Part III), with operational effectiveness and efficiency (although not Pareto optimality). But all of the foregoing must make it amply clear that he is concerned with power in many if not all of its diverse aspects. Schumpeter's central argument about capitalism, socialism, and democracy must be understood and critiqued in terms of power, and this I undertake in section II.

II. CRITIQUE

A. Schumpeter's Argument

The explicit argument of *Capitalism, Socialism, and Democracy* is quite subtle and complex: It is a defense of an allegedly historic capitalism, an extrapolation of capitalist decay and of socialist succession, and an analysis of how or why socialism not only can "work" but also function in a manner superior to modern capitalism.

Part I of the volume comprises a preliminary interpretation of Karl Marx as prophet, sociologist, economist, and teacher.

Part II is in many respects the heart of the book. Here we have a candid apologia for capitalism: It is an engine of mass production which has improved the living conditions of the masses. Instability and unemployment should not obscure the fact of secular real growth. Rejecting the stagnation argument, Schumpeter denies that investment opportunities are vanishing. He applauds the leadership selection process which has conditioned and selected simultaneously, rising and doing well being seen as one and the same thing. Furthermore, he envisions capitalism to be an evolutionary process of creative destruction in which the ultimate competition involves innovation rather than price.

There is here also an apologia for business bigness and restrictive practices. Monopolistic competition and oligopoly, not competition, characterize the modern capitalist economy, and certain restrictive practices actually may protect rather than impede secular expansion, for example, by providing secure investment expectations. Indeed, it is capitalist organization per se which is defended—against the claims of government action, gold, population increase, new land, and technological progress itself—as the principal force behind growth of output, indeed, the propelling force behind technological progress. Short-run competitive requirements are less important, to Schumpeter, than the factors making for long-run dynamics.

Capitalism, although it may have a century or so to run,[108] is, however, doomed to decay and to destroy itself, to die by virtue of its own achievements, due to several causes. First, the entrepreneurial function is becoming obsolescent due to the corporate routinization and specialization of innovation. Second, the protecting strata required for a bourgeois society to survive politically are being destroyed, as is the institutional framework of capitalist society. Third, the capitalist system abets the development of rationalist habits of mind which tend to become critical habits of mind. A principal vehicle of this rationalism and criticalism is the intellectual. As a consequence of these developments, the position of the entrepreneur, indeed, of the capitalists and bourgeoisie as a whole, is weakened. The habits of loyalty and of super- and subordination essential to the working of the system are destroyed. Capitalist values lose their hold on both the public mind and the capitalist strata. The business class is increasingly unable to defend itself, much less to rule. Rising real incomes, the modern corporation (a product of business rationalism which socializes the bourgeois mind, narrowing and devitalizing bourgeois motivation), and rationalism paradoxically result in the disintegration and decomposition of capitalist society. These developments "make not only for the destruction of the capitalist but for the emergence of a socialist civilization."[109]

Part III argues—regrettably, as it were, to Schumpeter—that socialism, understood as central economic control, can work. Central decision makers can organize and administer production. Although planners' preferences are likely to be substituted for consumers' preference, markets and prices can be used to introduce and implement consistent, rational, maximizing decisions. Indeed, Schumpeter argues that socialist organization not only need not break down but also would proceed very much along the lines of the increasingly large capitalist firms, which he sees as already a step toward socialism.[110]

In matters of comparative efficiency, Schumpeter admonishes his reader, socialism is to be compared with monopoly capitalism, not competition. Accordingly, the socialist blueprint may be superior: a less wasteful adjustment process, the elimination of cyclical instability, and an end to the wastage of resources in economic warfare and the struggle to control government economic policy. As for the human element, no fundamental reform of human nature is necessary for socialism to work. Bureaucratic management, necessary for socialism, is far advanced under capitalism. Labor discipline, as we have seen, likely will be an easier task under socialism than in capitalism. Social saving and investment, of course, can be centrally managed. Transition to socialism will be facilitated if capitalist society has matured, that is, if the economic process largely has socialized the human soul and the means of production through concentration of ownership in corporate business, if depersonalization and the wilting away of capitalist motivation and standards have taken place, and so on. Socialization in a state of immaturity is not impossible but more difficult and likely to be more wild.

In Part IV we have Schumpeter's argument that the classical doctrine of democracy, namely, that the common good and the popular will prevail, is empirically wrong; that democracy is essentially a competition for political leadership. He concludes, in accordance with his theory of democracy, that there is no necessary relation between democracy and socialism, especially no incompatibility, although socialist democracy "may eventually turn out to be more of a sham than capitalist democracy ever was."[111]

Part V is a historical sketch of socialist parties, governments, and policies from roughly 1875 into the post–World War II period. Most of this discussion is not directly relevant to my analysis, although several points are worth noting. He says that Marxism has been unrealistic and utopian in identifying with the proletariat rather than with the bureaucracy and politicians.[112] He also says that socialist parties in office have been generally successful, if precariously situated; their fundamental problem has been that they have been governing an essentially capitalist society and economy, that is, administering capitalism.[113] Among other things, the chapter Schumpeter added after World War II remarked that even before the war expropriation of the upper income backets in the United States had so tremendously transferred wealth that "the present distribution of disposable incomes compares well with the one actually prevailing in Russia."[114]

The famous "March into Socialism" reiterates the basic argument of the original book, adding both that inflation will accelerate the process of decay and that certain remedies (tight money and increased incidence of taxation on consumption) will likely only prolong the period before capitalism eventually breaks down.

I want now, forty years after the initial publication of the book and *perhaps prematurely*, to critique Schumpeter's central argument. What does it mean for Schumpeter to have said that capitalism is killing itself? Is capitalism being replaced by socialism and, if so, in what sense? Depending upon how we interpret reality and Schumpeter, he may have been right or wrong.

I do not propose to consider what Schumpeter *really* meant. I am prepared to take his words and argument at face value. I do want to question his interpretative base and his specific interpretation of systemic evolution. I believe that Schumpeter had a very narrow view of "capitalism" and that this colored his perception, interpretation, and argument.

B. Capitalism? Socialism?

It will be recalled that when Schumpeter presents his definition of the society and economy to which he more typically refers as capitalism he calls it a "commercial society." By this he means an institutional pattern of which he mentions only two elements, "private property in means of production and regulation of the productive process by private contract (or management of initiative)." At this point, capitalism is said to be a special case of commercial society, "defined by the additional phenomenon of credit creation." He says that in modern society the difference is unimportant "since commercial society, as an alternative to socialism, in practice always appears in the particular form of capitalism." Thus he largely (but not entirely) keeps to the "traditional contrast between capitalism and socialism."[115] Schumpeter does nothing else with these taxonomic niceties, and his distinctions are superfluous to his argument. For present purposes, Schumpeterian capitalism definitionally involves private ownership of the means of production and regulation of the productive process by private contract (or, as he says, management or initiative).

Elsewhere Schumpeter says a great deal more about the nature and meaning of capitalism. There is a capitalist "order,"[116] a capitalist "society,"[117] a capitalist "regime."[118] Capitalism is a system in which the dominant position is held and enjoyed by the capitalist class.[119] It is a system of business leadership,[120] a system of essentially bourgeois power. Its true form is unfettered capitalism.[121] Capitalism is not merely a system of consumer sovereignty. It is, rather, "a scheme of values, an attitude toward life, a civilization—the civilization of inequality and of the family fortune" and accumulation.[122] Capitalism is a system in which private property and free contract form "the moral horizon of the people."[123] Success is reckoned in terms of business success.[124] When he writes of the "organic conditions of a capitalist economy," Schumpeter specifies the "high premia on industrial success and all the other inequalities of income that may be required in order to make the capitalist engine work according to design."[125] The operative motives are the "promises of wealth and the threats of destitution."[126] He writes of the entrepreneurial function of the bourgeoisie as the function to which it has owed its social weight.[127] Capitalism therefore is a system of order, or rule, in the interests of the capitalists (or entrepreneurs or bourgeoisie) as those interests are defined by their definition of reality and their value system. More specifically, capitalism is the system and the world of the individualist entrepreneur,[128] and its demise is the demise of the individualist entrepreneur and his class.[129]

Schumpeter's treatment of the meaning and nature of capitalism raises fundamental questions, questions which go far beyond the taxonomy of commercial and capitalist society and the precise relation between capitalist, entrepreneur, and bourgeoisie. Schumpeter, it appears to me, had a quite narrow conception of capitalism in at least two respects, one of which is profoundly important for evaluating his interpretation of the demise of capitalism.

First, there is a serious question as to whether capitalism

is a system in which only, or principally, capitalist interests, conceptions of the world, and values dominate. Several specific issues arise in this connection. Is the underlying reality *capitalism* (by whatever definition) or *market economy*? Is the only market economy a capitalist economy? Can a market (or capitalist) economy by organized with varying sets of institutions? Can there be a pluralistic capitalist, or market, economy? Does capitalism (or the market economy) require a hierarchically superior position for business—the catering to the felt needs of, definition of social purpose by, and understanding of means-ends relations by business? Apropos of Schumpeter himself, given his emphasis on leadership, was it inevitable that he would stress the reality of a *capitalist* rather than a *market* economy and of individualist entrepreneurs rather than businessmen generally? What is the significance of his italicized reference to a "*laborist capitalism*"?[130] These are important matters, but I shall not dwell upon them; I think there is another and presently more important question involved in appraising his argument. But having said this, let me not appear to denigrate the first question. Whether Schumpeter's conception of capitalism prejudges the possibility of a non-business-dominated, more pluralistic market (but still capitalist) economy is not a trivial matter and certainly enters into the significance which we attribute to my second question.

The second question, one more directly relevant to Schumpeter's own argument, is whether individualist entrepreneurial capitalism is the only form of capitalism properly considered such, limiting capitalism only to a system of the predominant position of business and businessmen. The crux of Schumpeter's analysis is the decline of the old individual entrepreneurial capitalism. When that has passed, is capitalism dead? Schumpeter, of course, seems to mean precisely this. But I think we are entitled to ask several questions. These involve, ultimately, definitions, but the conceptions ensconced in the definitions govern our interpretation of reality. Thus the questions are not merely semantic; they penetrate to the definition of reality posited by Schumpeter's understanding of capitalism as individualist entrepreneurial capitalism and thereby to his argument concerning the demise of capitalism.

Cannot capitalism be seen as more than solely individualist entrepreneurial capitalism? Is the opposite of (or successor to) that kind of capitalism—the diffused, private, family-based entrepreneurial control of production—only central state control of production? What of the system of giant, perhaps conglomerate, perhaps multinational, corporations—the *corporate system*? Is not the corporate system a system of business control no less than that of the individualist entrepreneur? Does not the prestige motive for acquiring money and private wealth operate in the corporate system?[131] Does not the "most glamorous of . . . bourgeois aims, the foundation of an industrial dynasty"[132] find its realization in the corporate system? Is not the standard of accumulation, vis-à-vis the standard of consumption, alive in the corporate system? Are not those "organic conditions of a capitalist economy, including high premia on industrial success and all the other inequalities of income"[133] found in the corporate system? Schumpeter emphasizes the "cultural indeterminateness of socialism," that socialism can have many possible forms and institutionalizations;[134] but is there not a cultural indeterminateness of capitalism, too, in the same sense?

Before considering the significance of the corporate system for Schumpeter's argument, let us again review his intended meaning of "socialism." In the passage in which he defines commercial (or capitalist) society, it will be recalled, Schumpeter defines socialist society as "an institutional pattern in which the control over means of production and over production itself is vested with a central authority—or, as we may say, in which, as a matter of principle, the economic affairs of society belong to the public and not to the private sphere."[135] Schumpeter goes out of his way to cast aside considerations of both *state* ownership and the precise structure of central decision making,[136] and he rejects definitions or connotations of socialism which are too wide.[137] Having defined capitalism in terms of private ownership, he may be chided for finessing the question of state or public ownership (for example, if "public" does not mean "state," then what does it mean?), particularly in light of the questions I shall raise below concerning the nature of the corporate system. There are significant hiatuses here; most people have equated public with state and both with socialism in interpreting Schumpeter's central argument.

Schumpeter also seems often to consider welfare-state resource allocation, regulation, and such matters as socialist, although here he may be excused for lapsing into the mindsets of his readers and, especially, of the politicians and theorists whose ideas and policies he describes (especially in Part V and the two appended pieces). More confusing, however, than the possible ambiguities introduced by such usages is the wording adopted in the second paragraph of "The March into Socialism":

> I define (centralist) socialism as that organization of society in which the means of production are controlled, and the decisions on how and what to produce and on who is to get what, are made by public authority instead of by privately-owned and privately-managed firms. All that we mean by the March into Socialism is, therefore, the migration of people's economic affairs from the private into the public sphere.[138]

There are two problems here. First, if the alternative to privately managed firms is socialism, then where does the corporation enter? It is privately owned, but does Schumpeter restrict private ownership to individualist entrepreneurial ownership? Second, earlier[139] socialism was defined exclusively in centralist terms; here we have the possibility of a noncentralist socialism. But perhaps Schumpeter's parenthetic insertion was intended only to emphasize that public authority was centralist, at least in juxtaposition to a dispersed private, capitalist economy. (But what of a *concentrated* ownership in nominally private corporations?) At both places, central control is stressed, and the distinction also is made between private and public spheres, although the capitalism-socialism distinction is made ambiguous by his declining to specify socialism in terms of public ownership and by his apparent neglect of the situation of central control which also is nominally private (the corporate system). By socialism, then, Schumpeter seems to have meant central public-sector control of production and distribution. This seems to connote *effective* public control, if not ownership, of the means of production and central planning (*vide* his discussion of determinate, consistent, rational production decisions).[140]

What, then, is the reality which, as Schumpeter envisioned it, was replacing individualist entrepreneurial capitalism? Schumpeter's argument, it will be recalled, is that the facts seem (regrettably) to indicate the inevitability of socialism—that is, that the factors making for the transformation or destruction of (individualist entrepreneurial) capitalism are the same factors making for the emergence of socialist civilization.[141] The apparently inevitable (although not necessarily proximate) decomposition of capitalism and emergence of socialism provide, after all, the reason for inquiring, in Part III of the book, whether socialism can work.

But notice the reality which Schumpeter describes in his discussion of the crumbling and decomposition of capitalism: the obsolescence of the entrepreneurial function, the destruction of the protecting strata, and the destruction of the institutional framework of capitalist society (as well as growing hostility to the system itself, which I discuss separately below). What we have here, in part, is the growth of the corporation, especially the giant corporation, the predominance of monopolistic competition and oligopoly (not that capitalism ever evidenced perfect competition),[142] and the corporate bureaucratization and routinization of the entrepreneurial function. The modern corporation, it is his central thesis, socializes the bourgeois mind and property[143] as well as business risk.[144] It ousts the bourgeoisie (or the entrepreneurs in their midst) from the function to which they have owed their social weight.[145] Business is increasingly controlled by a small number of bureaucratized corporations in which progress is mechanized and planned.[146]

So the old individualist entrepreneurial system is being replaced by a corporate system, quite independent of the critiques of hostile intellectuals. I think that we are entitled to ask several questions. Can we not see individualist entrepreneurial capitalism as but a stage[147] in the development of capitalism—perhaps, but not necessarily, a stage preparatory or transitional to "true" capitalism, or at least to the next stage, corporate capitalism? Can we not recognize the corporate system as a new form of capitalism—different but still capitalist—as a system of business control and organization of the economy? Can we not distinguish between the entrepreneurial function and the old entrepreneurial class, between the entrepreneurial function and the group in which its performance is located? Can we not recognize the corporate system and the new business-leader group as the successor to the old individualist entrepreneurial elite? Is not Schumpeter's interpretation infused with an individualist ideology now largely eclipsed by the corporate system and the new managerialist ideology[148] (however much the latter has vestiges of individualist ideology, which, after all, remain useful for social control)? Does not Schumpeter's idealization of capitalism in terms of the individualist, familistic entrepreneur suggest, vis-à-vis the business leadership of the corporate system, an intermediate or transitional stage combining the familial, dynastic element of the old aristocracy and the entrepreneurial function of the new economic system? Along a quite different line, may not Schumpeter's rejection of competition theory, individualist ideology, and classical democratic theory, each as absent from the modern economy, serve to contribute to the destruction of certain idea-systems useful, after a fashion, as a check on the corporate system and on the power of business generally?

What I am suggesting, then, is that *by Schumpeter's own account*, individualist entrepreneurial capitalism and public-sector control of production and distribution are not the only alternatives. By his own account, the corporate system seems to be a third alternative, the capitalist successor to individualist entrepreneurial capitalism.

But this line of reasoning raises further questions as to the nature of capitalism, socialism, and the corporate system itself. Is the modern corporate system capitalist or socialist? From the perspective of the historical individualist entrepreneurial system it may well appear collectivist, or socialist. From the perspective of the public ownership–central planning socialist it may well appear individualist and capitalist. We can see the corporate system as a version of central planning—a system of private planning, more or less effectively centralized—*or* as a capitalist sequel to individualist entrepreneurial capitalism—a successor evolutionary form of bourgeois or business power. If socialism can be perceived as state capitalism, the corporate system can be seen as private socialism. Indeed, Schumpeter himself perceived certain developments in capitalist economies as steps toward socialism.[149] If a Howard Hughes owned and/or controlled the Fortune 500 (or some suitably large proportion of it), would not the management of his portfolio, in all its ramifications, constitute a system of planning, "private socialism"? Corporate concentration, planning, and coordinated activity can be seen as a step toward socialism, as socialism itself (albeit in the guise of the imagery of private property), or as an alternative to socialism. Certainly neither Soviet imperative nor French indicative planning are conclusive or exhaustive as to the possibilities of "planning." In recent years John Kenneth Galbraith,[150] Arthur S. Miller,[151] Charles E. Lindblom,[152] and Edward S. Herman,[153] not to neglect Walter Adams,[154] John Blair,[155] and Daniel Fusfeld,[156] among others, have described central control-planning through diversification, conglomeration, joint ventures, financial groups, and so on, as not the least of the various symbiotic relationships with government (see below).

It may very well be that the capitalism-socialism and private-public dichotomies are irrelevant. The further labeling of the corporate system as capitalist or socialist is not the important issue. The critical question, *if we are to follow Schumpeter*, concerns the distribution of power; leadership in and the power structure of the corporate system.

If we can dispense with the trappings of Schumpeter's argument in terms of capitalism and socialism, it seems to me both possible and necessary to settle on his emphasis on hierarchy—leadership—as key. Schumpeter's (positive) argument ultimately involves a change in the leadership strata of economy and society. I do not mean solely a change from capitalist to socialist leadership as those terms have been (more or less ambiguously) conventionally used, for Schumpeter does not discuss only the eviction of bourgeois by socialist leaders. Schumpeter, in his discussion of the apparent demise of capitalism (Part II), focuses on what may be perceived as a new and different leadership stratum within capitalist society—different and new in that it is the corporate administrator succeeding the individualist entrepreneur, but still nominally capitalist. More to the point, there is a distinctly new leadership-selection process. Much less a critical factor is the luck of family birth and connection; now it is increasingly (but not totally) the selection mechanisms of the corporate meritocracy (including the training and socializing processes of higher education for business).

Moreover, it may very well be that the new system is better able to absorb vigorous leadership material than the old (which may have had the defects of the old system of political rule by aristocratic-monarchical families). It also may very well be that the new business elite may be stronger than the old: It may not require protection from the old aristocratic hierarchy.

With leadership and leadership selection so important to Schumpeter, it is not insignificant to stress that the corporate system may represent only a different system of business leadership selection. The new upper strata, it is true, are managerialist and bureaucratic rather than old-style individualist businessmen, but they are businessmen manning the positions of a business elite and enjoying the privileged position of business.[157] They also have an elitist universal-manager perspective concerning the use, control, and discipline of the human labor force, a situation dramatically underscored when placed in juxtaposition to a system of labor management or participation with selection through the ranks of workers (which nonetheless may develop a cadre of "professional" or specialized worker-managers). The new system is, generally, every bit as hierarchic a system as the old, granted with a differently specifiable capitalist configuration or leadership-personnel selection mechanism. Paradoxically, it also is one which can more or less precisely qualify as a system of central control, especially if we follow Schumpeter and cast aside consideration of the precise structure of central decision making. Be that as it may, we are left with a system with a hierarchically dominant group and the interests which it will promote. As Galbraith and others might put it, we have the managerial class (in contrast to the individualist entrepreneur class) in a "new" hierarchical (corporate) system, whether perceived as capitalist or socialist.

This line of reasoning is supported by at least two further themes present in *Capitalism, Socialism and Democracy*. One, of course, is Schumpeter's identification of and lament about increasingly fettered (individualist entrepreneurial) capitalism, for example, consumer- and labor-oriented reforms. These fetters restrict the ability of the entrepreneur to perform his function. Schumpeter believed that success of the capitalist engine requires the (individualist entrepreneurial) capitalists to be left alone to perform their important function.

The second theme warrants close attention. It involves Schumpeter's judgment that in the (new) system of central economic control (which I am suggesting could be historical socialism or the corporate system) economic management should similarly be insulated from political interference. At first blush, this seems awkward, if not ironic: If the central authority (however itself structured) in control of production and distribution is in the public sphere, indeed if there is central control of production and distribution, is not that *ipso facto* government and "political"? As we shall see, whatever one thinks of Schumpeter's attitude toward and portrayal of "socialism" versus (individualist entrepreneurial) "capitalism," his most evident and revealing antagonism is toward politics, politicians, and the state, but especially that which he perceived as politics and politicians. The matter warrants development in some detail.

First, let me note that Schumpeter did consider and affirm the necessity of a professional political stratum, that is, professionally developed politicians vis-à-vis political amateurs—in other words, an independent political class. Thus, in discussing the need to secure "politicians of sufficiently good quality," he says that "experience seems to suggest that the only effective guarantee is in the existence of a social stratum, itself a product of a severely selective process, that takes to politics as a matter of course. If such a stratum be neither too exclusive nor too easily accessible for the outsider and if it be strong enough to assimilate most of the elements it currently absorbs, it not only will present for the political career products of stocks that have successfully passed many tests in other fields—served, as it were, an apprenticeship in private affairs—but it will also increase their fitness by endowing them with traditions that embody experience, with a professional code and with a common fund of views."[158]

More important, however, is the need to insulate economic decision makers (economic managers) from political decision makers (political managers):

> The essential point to grasp is this. No responsible person can view with equanimity the consequences of extending the democratic method, that is to say the sphere of "politics," to all economic affairs. Believing that democratic socialism means precisely this, such a person will naturally conclude that demo-

> cratic socialism must fail. But this does not necessarily follow. As has been pointed out before, extension of the range of public management does not imply corresponding extension of the range of political management. Conceivably, the former may be extended so as to absorb a nation's economic affairs while the latter still remains within the boundaries set by the limitations of the democratic method.
>
> . . . the agencies that are to operate the economic engine—the Central Board . . . as well as the subordinate bodies entrusted with the management of individual industries or concerns—may be so organized and manned as to be sufficiently exempt in their fulfillment of their current duties from interference by politicians or, for that matter, by fussing citizens' committees or by their workmen.[159]

Moreover,

> It is not enough that the bureaucracy should be efficient in current administration and competent to give advice. It must also be strong enough to guide and, if need be, to instruct the politicians who head the ministries. In order to be able to do this it must be in a position to evolve principles of its own and sufficiently independent to assert them. It must be a power in its own right.[160]

Substitute corporate management for public management in that analysis and one has the attitude of corporate managers toward government and toward (organized) labor. Schumpeter's managerial class, broadly conceived, may be understood to include both economic and political managers, but his stress is on the relative operational independence of the economic managers. As has been the case in historical capitalism, the upper economic strata are to be left to do their things, to exercise and administer central economic control, however it is structured. It seems to me that, notwithstanding obvious and normatively important differences, Schumpeter was empirically correct insofar as he may be understood as having emphasized the creation of a managerial leadership group more or less insulated from the vagaries of political competition, in both nominally capitalist and socialist societies (but a group engaging, of course, in symbiosis with the official political leadership).

Schumpeter wanted the central economic managers insulated from politics. He also believed that decisions could be made on technical grounds; indeed, it was for that reason that the central economic managers were to be "left alone." In the new system, all sorts of economic decisions, if not all economic decisions other than personal ones—such as "the relations between agriculture and industry, small-scale and large-scale industry, steel-producing and steel-consuming industries, protectionist and export industries"—"will—or may—cease to be political questions to be settled by the relative weights of pressure groups and become technical questions to which technicians would be able to give unemotional and unequivocal answers."[161]

I think that Schumpeter was both wrong and realistic with regard to insulated, technically based decision making. It is not true that the important decisions are technical. There are technical elements, but allocation (and other) decisions are subjective and normative, a function in large part of whose interests are to count, in part through the antecedent, often implicit, normative premises of policy analysts and decision makers, and that involves politics, however labeled or buried. Decision making cannot be insulated from politics; it *is* politics. But Schumpeter is instructive, perhaps correct, in several respects.

First, there is a strong tendency for economic managers, in both nominally capitalist and socialist regimes, to seek autonomy and control over technical decision making.

Second, the ideas of necessary insulation and technically based decisions are functional in isolating and legitimizing the decision-making elite. Whether we call the corporate system capitalist or socialist, it is manned largely by technocrats—and their historical rationalization, now more clearly seen, is in terms of (a) individualism, (b) competitive market, and (c) managerialism, however disparate these seemingly are.[162]

Third, the reality of the situation is evidenced, for example, by the conflict among public finance specialists as to whether public expenditure (and taxation) decisions involve significantly technical rather than ideological issues and whether there are conclusive principles for technicians to apply.[163] The point, of course, is that there are continued conflicts over "technical" solutions, only they become increasingly buried in or obscured by the formal apparatus and techniques of "decision making," such as benefit-cost analysis and optimal control.[164] Schumpeter's critique of rationalism ironically must be juxtaposed to his emphasis on technicians and technical solutions; Schumpeter is the ultimate rationalist. His striking comment that it would have been less visionary and more realistic for socialists to have identified with the bureaucracy and politicians ("governments or . . . classes other than the proletariat")[165]reinforces the lesson of this reasoning. Schumpeter was less interested, notwithstanding the formal framework of the book, in capitalism-socialism than in the vitality and viability of the ruling managerial elite. I suspect that he did not fail to comprehend the political element in technical solutions. He rather thought (or hoped?) that any modern successor to the traditional European aristocracy would be more fit to rule than were the uninstructed and otherwise unequipped masses who might be brought to power through the vagaries of democratic politics, however defined. His fundamental elitism seems to have obscured even from him the real thrust of his argument as to the future of capitalism and socialism, which is much more directed to the nature and circumstances of the upper strata of society in whose hands rest the long-run interests of society, that is, whose decisions largely define the long-run interests of society.

One final aspect of this is worth noting. Schumpeter's candor led him to recognize that the classical and neoclassical theorem on the profit motive, that perfect competition tends to maximize production, requires assumptions which reduce the principle to "little more than a truism."[166] But for all that Schumpeter was no less taken with "maximum performance in production."[167]

To him the "capitalist engine is first and last an engine of mass production which unavoidably means also production for the masses."[168] His evaluative criterion was production. Anything which impaired the conditions of further economic development—meaning greater production of output—was suspect.[169] This is true of Schumpeter even though he also recognized, in the manner perhaps of Thorstein Veblen, that "production is incidental to the making or profits."[170] But production of what? If production is incidental to the making of profits, it is the judgments and determinations of those seeking profit which help govern what output is to be produced; these also help govern the cultural influence of those persons or strata as to what output is worth having in everyone's style of life. The relevant critical question in society involves the forces which help determine whether the output of an industry is to be defined in terms of its physical product or some combination thereof with investor profits, managerial lifetime incomes, worker safety, and so on. The same is true regarding social policy as to any necessary trade-off between greater physical output (or greater output however defined) and alterations of social (for example, property) structure. The point is that different implicit decisions as to output definitions and social policy will be made if ruling strata change. It is they who define the long-run interests of society, which includes the definition of outputs. It is precisely these definitions which are at stake in more mundane conflicts over the welfare state, particularly at the numerous points where the perceived interests of the corporate system conflict with those of other groups (for example, workers, consumers, and the disadvantaged).

C. Government and the Economy

I already have suggested that Schumpeter must be given mixed grades regarding his treatment of the economic role of government. On the one hand, he often candidly focuses on the importance of government and penetrates to very deep legal-economic fundamentals. On the other hand, his treatment frequently is infused with and made myopic by what we may call either his immediate involvements in economic organizations, operation, and performance. Having discussed his inconsistent recognition of the legal foundations of capitalism and of capitalist domination and use of government, having stressed the inadequacies of the public-private dichotomy, and having suggested that the corporate system may be considered a system of private planning, or private socialism, I want to complete my analysis in these matters.

Let me preface these points by referring to comments made by the conservative political columnist George Will on a widely quoted statement by President Ronald Reagan in an address to the Congress shortly after taking office. Reagan said: "The taxing power of government must . . . not be used to regulate the economy or bring about social change." Will's comments are both pithy and very instructive:

> Oh? The choice of any tax program is a choice from a large universe of alternatives. Any tax program has special social consequences; it raises some revenues rather than others, encourages and discourages particular behavior. And rarely has there been a clearer, bolder, more self-conscious attempt than Reagan's to use the tax system as a lever for moving society in the direction of desired change. But American conservatives are addicted to the pose of hostility to government power, so they systematically misdescribe their attempt to use government energetically.
>
> When, Oh Lord, shall we be delivered from the conservatives' pretense that they, unlike liberals, do not believe in using government to promote their values through social change? If that were true, there would be no point in electing conservatives.[171]

Without attempting any particular hypothesis or implication as to the mix, in the real world, of deliberate pretense, naivete, and inadvertent myopia, I think that Will is correct with regard to the reality of the socioeconomic uses and consequences of government. Ideology aside, the question always is not whether government is involved, but which interests government is to be used to support.[172]

Apropos of *Capitalism, Socialism, and Democracy*, I would make several points. First, the fundamental issues are not capitalism versus socialism but (1) the identity and (2) vitality of the hierarchical distribution of power and (3) the exercise of that hierarchical power with regard to the control and use of government (in part, with respect to the control and discipline of the human labor force). The one relevant question society must resolve is to which interests will government lend its support, that is, which class or group interests will government seek to promote.

Second, Schumpeter simply is not consistent in his recognition of the continuing contest for the control of government. If one wishes to be more charitable in that regard, then one is forced to acknowledge that Schumpeter often was simply influenced by his bourgeois biases and blinders. Although he sometimes penetrates to the heart of the legal-economic nexus and to bourgeois dominance of the state, he does not consistently follow through with these perceptions. Accordingly, his deep insights into legal-economic reality are often blurred by interpretations and/or applications made from a bourgeois, or individualist entrepreneur, perspective. Thus, he both identifies and obscures the problem of who is to use government and for what purposes. He mixes a recognition of the positive use of the state made by the bourgeoisie with their negative view of the state. He also takes an elitist view of the contest for the control and use of government. This contest fundamentally involves the distribution of use between (and among) the upper hierarchical levels and the rest of society, the use consisting of making and remaking law to alter the distribution of opportunities for different groups in society, the contest taking place typically over the terms on which each class or group is to use the state to its own advantage. This governance of the course of legal change is the most fundamental and recondite form of economic planning. In this Schumpeter typically assumed the perspective of the upper hierarchical groups. Schumpeter's treatment is illustrated by his selective invocaton of the creative destruction theme: He uses it to legitimize business-produced change and, indirectly, to rationalize legal change in favor of business and to oppose legal change desired by other groups in society. Schumpeter was aware, it would appear, of the magnitude and role of myths and deception in society—the pretended absolutes of various economic systems—as alleged preconditions for, say, economic growth; but (a) he was not always able (or self-motivated) to transcend them, and (b) he seems to have envisioned himself as a high-level systems manager using them to effectuate goals which he deemed desirable.

Thus, Schumpeter seems either not to have seen or to have given quite inadequate attention to the fact that the entrepreneurial and the corporate system each constitutes a different legal-economic nexus, but both are systems of business domination of government, and each is but a different form of business-government symbiosis. Alternatively, he simply took same for granted. He does seem to have failed to recognize, either at all or as constituting capitalism, two important factors. There were, first, the performance by the corporate system of the planning function in symbiosis with government (for example, as outlined in Galbraith's *New Industrial State*) and, second, the efforts of big business to control the state to limit and channel the gales of creative destruction in their interests.[173]

Finally, Schumpeter was uncomfortable with the fact that business has had to share its control and use of government with other, nonelite groups; accordingly, trade-offs have had to be made between business interests and the various interests of consumers and workers ensconced in the welfare state with regard to the conditions of the use and discipline of the human labor force and the definition of output—that is to say, with regard to the definition of social purpose. This does point, however, to a fundamental lesson which can be distilled from *Capitalism, Socialism, and Democracy*: The contest for the control and use of government is instrumental to the contest for the control and use of the human labor force. It is, after all, both these contests with respect to which hierarchy is "all about."[174]

D. Rationalism and the Intellectuals

Schumpeter's treatment of rationalism and the intellectuals is not so much wrong as considerably incomplete. Rationalism, it will be recalled, he identified as yielding criticism of the capitalist status quo, and the intellectuals he characterized as the uprooted, alienated critics. I want to make a number of points in these connections.

First, as I have indicated, Schumpeter himself is eminently rationalist in his demythologizing, his approach to socialism, and his emphasis on the ostensible objectivity and conclusivity of technical solutions. These clearly are manifestations, perhaps extreme, of rationalism—although Schumpeter was a blend of realist, rationalist, and romantic.[175]

Second, rationalism is a much more encompassing phenomenon than capitalism. There also is much more to the relations between capitalism and rationalism than rationalist criticism of capitalism. Schumpeter's lament at the rise of the anticapitalist mentality oddly seems to assume that once upon a time there had been none. In actuality, rationalism has produced critiques of pre- and non-bourgeois forms of society as well as capitalism; Western society was never completely bourgeois; antimodernism (anticapitalism, anti-industrialism, and anti-urbanism) was rampant in the nineteenth century, indeed since the earlier recognitions of modernism, and such criticism, some rationalist and some romanticist, has come from both left and right; and rationalism itself has been held to be a source of domination and exploitation.[176] Furthermore, although Schumpeter identifies rationalism as the product of capitalism, and although capitalism admittedly has reinforced rationalist tendencies, capitalism may be seen to be much more a product of rationalism than vice versa. Criticism of capitalism from "within" capitalist society is every bit as modern as rationalist capitalism itself (and the rationalist businessman). Finally, by the way of comparison, it must be remembered that Max Weber understood that capitalism not only signified rational bureaucracy in the service of pecuniary profit but also that capitalist enterprise could vary in its modes of capitalist ideals, forms of markets, types of property structures, working procedures (including ways of assigning rank and responsibility), and the political and military environments within which it could operate. Also, Werner Sombart's understanding of capitalism included both the adventurous, risk-assuming, and acquisitive spirit of enterprise and the rational, disciplined, and risk-calculating bourgeois (or burgher) spirit. Apropos of Sombart, interestingly, in a 1912 book Schumpeter distinguished "hedonic-static" and "dynamic-energetic" types of economic conduct.[177]

With regard to Schumpeter's treatment of the intellectuals, I want to make several additional points. First, Schumpeter engages in probably unconscious selective perception and identification of intellectuals: Critical intellects are intellectuals, but not all critics are intellectuals, and not all intellectuals are critics. Intellectuals are homogeneous as to neither ideas nor allegiances.

Second, Schumpeter's own rationalism and candor has seemed elitist (and to constitute nascent or subtle socialism) to his right-wing critics. But, ironically, some of the most conservative defenders of the present system, in their application of the utilitarian analysis of neoclassical economics to institutions hitherto perceived as nonutilitarian in their operation and evolution (such as the family), may contribute to the destruction of capitalism's institutional base and thereby constitute a manifestation of and/or contribution to the decomposition of capitalism.[178]

Third, Schumpeter blames the intellectuals for their contribution to the decomposition of capitalism. When one considers that their rationalist habit of mind is attributed by Schumpeter to capitalism itself, this attribution of blame seems ill-directed. It is made more odd when it is remembered that businessmen and big business itself are, to Schumpeter, rationalist products of capitalism, and that capitalism would appear doomed, by Schumpeter's own analysis, even without the criticism by the intellectuals. Capitalism, after all, is seen to be destroying itself—and both businessmen and intellectuals are endogenous, not exogenous, to the system of capitalism. Blaming the manifestations or vehicles of this self-destruction—or only some of them—seems at least awkward. Schumpeter's own analysis is much more complex and subtle than his scapegoating of intellectuals recognizes or gives effect to. Along a different line, but to the same effect, Schumpeter presents the case for "monopoly capitalism." Why cannot *that* be seen as destructive of the "civilization of capitalism"? Along a still different line, his anti-intellectual stance seems ironical inasmuch as it is the intellectuals who, at least in part, will serve as the managerial elite of the new system, whether it be seen as corporate capitalism or socialism (or anything else). Moreover, certainly Schumpeter's criticism of rationalism and the intellectuals is less fundamental and ubiquitous in his notion of economic reality than are the contests over the control and use of the human labor force and the state, with his criticism of the intellectuals seemingly functioning as a stratagem in those matters.[179]

Fourth, Schumpeter surely did not intend to rule out of bounds all criticism of any status quo. One raison d'etre of the book is a critique of capitalism, socialism, and democracy. His rejection of the classical theory of democracy and his assertion that socialism can work seem to qualify as such a critique. In addition, one can surmise that Schumpeter would have welcomed (some or all of) the criticism by intellectuals of the noncapitalist regimes of Eastern Europe.

Fifth, Schumpeter was very much aware[180] that socioeconomic policy was a product of social choice (however much that choice resided in the hands of upper hierarchic levels and their political and bureaucratic underlings) and that such choice was a product, in part, of a contest over the minds—over the definitions of reality and values—of active persons. Another reason for writing the book clearly was to influence those minds.

E. Schumpeter's Theory of Democracy

Schumpeter rejected the classical theory of democracy (which he recognized as bourgeois in origin), with its emphasis on the common good and the popular will, and proposed a theory of competition for political leadership. Apropos thereof, I want to make certain points without much elaboration.

First, as a positive, descriptive matter, Shumpeter's theory seems to me to be generally empirically correct—or at least a necessary major qualification to the classical theory (itself requiring qualification; see below). His theory requires amplification, or modification, to bring to bear considerable research and theorizing on politics, government, political parties, and so on, but his theory seems to be often more empirically useful in explaining and understanding political reality in a world of hierarchical power structures than is the classical theory.

Second, as I have indicated above, the theory of democracy as a competition for political leadership, if it is to be useful for purposes of explanation and understanding, must be allowed to lead to a theory of a contest to control the use of the state. Political leadership, after all, is leadership in use of government.

Third, if the notion of a corporate system (however labeled) is appropriate, then it should be useful to explore further corporate control of government, government-business symbiosis, and the concept of a corporate state complementary to that of a corporate system.

Fourth, Schumpeter's theory of democracy must be understood in conjunction with his emphasis, examined above, on technical solutions to problems of policy made by an insulated, if not isolated managerial elite.

Fifth, the question of the relation between capitalism and democracy continues to be important and discussed.[181] A great deal depends, of course, on what one means by "capitalism" and "democracy" as well as on one's premises regarding underlying hierarchical social structures.

Sixth, to many the real problem would be self-government, even with leadership. After all, the origins of democracy—understood to mean popular government, popular participation in governance, self-government, or simply the more or less universal franchise—must be seen in juxtaposition to monarchical and aristocratic government. In this connection, I note the following points: (1) The ideology or myth of classical democratic theory may be useful to promote greater citizen opportunity for participation in governance. (2) Ideological emphasis on Schumpeter's definition, or on the necessity of limited democracy, may function only to reinforce hierarchical use of government. Alternatively stated, although his theory of democracy is empirically accurate, the theory has an independent political significance as argument functional for hierarchical alternatives to pluralism, that is, popular self-government. (3) As Schumpeter recognized and insisted,[182] the only effective guarantee of a high quality political stratum includes a sufficient measure of openness or accessibility. As Schumpeter expressed it, he envisioned "a stratum . . . neither too exclusive nor too easily accessible for the outsider and . . . strong enough to assimilate most of the elements it currently absorbs."[183] (4) The recent literature on governability, associated with an essay by Samuel P. Huntington,[184] raises questions not so much of excessive democracy but of identifying both the point of view from which ungovernability is perceived and identified and the power-oriented uses to which the ungovernability argument is put. The trappings of democracy sometimes provide a facade for authoritarian government.

Seventh, the masses long have engaged in a struggle whereby they, too, may use government for their self-perceived ends. Through the welfare state, for example, workers and others have sought to use democratic processes to create a society somewhat different from capitalism in either its individualist entrepreneur or corporate forms. What has evolved is a combination of the welfare state and the corporate system as a new form of capitalism. Schumpeter's analysis, as I have reinterpreted it, comes off well only with regard to the rise of the corporate system. The new corporate managerial class rose to systemic hegemony but not without paying the price of the welfare state. Democracy is broader and more complex and subtle, therefore, than Schumpeter acknowledges. John R. Commons's notion of democracy as the collective bargaining state, with politics engaged in between corporate and other groups, may be more accurate than Schumpeter's conception. (Neither notion may be close to the classical conception, though Common's is reflective of its spirit.) More generally, if democracy is understood to mean a wide diffusion of power with regard to the control of and use of government, democracy inevitably conflicts with the reality of and belief in hierarchical, concentrated power.

All in all, however, if one is prepared to make allowances for Schumpeter's elitism, his approach to matters of democratic government is instructive. (To say that, of course, does not commit one to any particular normative viewpoint, nor is it to say that Schumpeter's analysis is complete and correct in every detail.)[185] In part, it reinforces the interpretation that Schumpeter's analysis of capitalism-socialism results largely in pointing to the emergence of a new hierarchical stratum, whether nominally socialist or capitalist, whether in a system of private or public socialism. It is that stratum which will channel the use of government.

III. CONCLUSION

Joseph Schumpeter described what he believed to exist, and what was likely to exist, in *Capitalism, Socialism, and Democracy*. I believe that his analysis amounts to something quite different than he believed it did; that this different interpretation can be stated in terms manifestly Schumpeterian; and that, moreover, this alternative interpretation, at least with regard to the United States, is largely confirmed by experience, that is, by evolving economic reality as I interpret it.

Capitalism is not dying. (If the Western economies are threatened, it is due not to the factors ensconced in Schumpeter's analysis but to the relative success of Soviet imperialism as well as to blind greed.) Individual entrepreneurial capitalism largely has succumbed to corporate capitalism. Corporate capitalism is socialist only as private socialism, that is, as a new system of "private" central economic control with a new business-government symbiosis. More important, a new leadership stratum has been formed, with a new leadership selection process, and with a new set of business government interrelations (a new legal-economic nexus).

As it turned out, Schumpeter traced the development of the corporate system, the passing, not of capitalism, but of the old individualist entrepreneurial stage or form of capitalism.

Capitalism versus socialism – private versus public ownership of the means of production *or* private versus central economic control – may be irrelevant. Central economic control, in the form of business structure combined with government-business symbiosis quite different from formal planning, may exist in the corporate system and corporate state. Schumpeter's argument that socialism can work can be applied to the corporate system. Capitalist rationalism has produced the corporate system, and that system does produce determinate decisions as to production and distribution. What preferences exist and whose preferences count are other matters. There continues jockeying for power to control the human labor force. There continues the need to trade-off the perquisites of the managerial class, including its definition of output and social purpose, with the felt interests of consumers, workers, and others. All parties tend to be ambivalent as to the trade-off between more physical goods and services and other values, and the future and character of worker participation systems is problematic at best. More important than whether the extant system be denominated capitalism or socialism are other Schumpeterian concepts: hierarchy, leadership, leadership selection, discipline, and power.

Flawed though Schumpeter's analysis seems to be, it is nonetheless penetrating and enlightening. Perhaps somewhat inadvertently, Schumpeter's emphasis on technical solutions and insulated decision-making strata serves to underscore the empirical reality and importance of hierarchy and the managerial class. It also may be said, however, that Schumpeter's explicit focus on socialism has functioned, intentionally or inadvertently, to obscure the transformation of capitalism to its modern corporate form. It has done this by maintaining a definition of reality in which socialism is the only recognized alternative to (individualist entrepreneurial) capitalism.

Viewed in this light, it is not impossible to interpret the argument of *Capitalism, Socialism, and Democracy* as a more subtle and sophisticated defense of the classical theorem (which asserts that pursuit of private interest conduces to the realization of social interests) than the individualist, competitive paradigm of mainstream economics following the logic of the invisible hand. The greater subtlety and sophistication was required by the reality of oligopoly, unemployment, and concentrated (or centralized) economic power. It was provided by someone who identified with the elite of society, first the old aristocracy and then the old individualist entrepreneur. It would provide legitimacy for the new leadership selection process and the new leaders.

This is not the place to inquire into the predictive power of Schumpeter's argument, particularly various specifics. I have argued, of course, that if one understands that argument to have involved the corporate system replacing individualist entrepreneurial capitalism as a system of central economic control (in part through the symbiosis designated the "corporate state"), then, in my view, Schumpeter's argument, *thus understood or restated*, has borne up quite well. His strictures on other points also may have borne up well; several good examples are the requirement of maturity for successful socialization, the degenerating quality of democratic politics, the continued ability of capitalism to produce goods, and the severity of the inflation problem.

If one may speak of a final decision regarding capitalism, certainly one independent of international power politics and war, that decision may turn on the performance of its organization-and-control structure regarding stable, high employment and the distributions of income and wealth. To say this may impose excessively rationalist requirements on capitalism, but the alternative is a fatalism reinforcing the status quo hierarchy on its own power-surviving terms. Apropos of that hierarchy, we continue with the corporate system and corporate state symbiosis in which most decision making is rationalist and calculating, outside of public view, and typically obscure as to its real and actual, in contrast with its nominal or ostensible, purposes. Irregular innovation may be increasingly juxtaposed to regularity of employment. But neither Schumpeter nor any other economist has had an independent calculus by which to reach a decision. Such a decision is, in part, a matter of values, emotion, and so on. Schumpeter stressed capitalism as an engine of mass production; to have done so amounts, *inter alia*, to a choice equally as normative as one which stresses full employment stability. Schumpeter's argument was based in part on the latter (insofar as it is not a chimera) being a function of the former; John Maynard Keynes's, of course, was quite different.

As for where Schumpeter's analysis leaves economics, whether we accept his argument at face value or in the form of my reinterpretation, some of modern economics seems mythical, some functional as a defense of the emerging power structure, and some simply irrelevant. To the extent that the definition of socialism as central economic control is an applicable, if not accurate, interpretation of the corporate system, then the conventional market paradigm and defense of the present-day U.S. economy is severely limited, although not fully irrelevant. Surely, "market economy" means something different between the individualist entrepreneurial and corporate versions of that economy.

The questions Schumpeter raises explicitly and those his argument suggests deal with truly important matters regarding our understanding of economic reality. If these questions were thoroughly understood—I do not say fully and unanimously answered—politics and economics would be more sophisticated and illuminated, although probably much more nerve-racking. At least that is my view; Schumpeter likely would not agree. His reasons for disagreeing continue to inform us still.

NOTES

* I want to acknowledge the help provided by comments on an earlier draft by James F. Becker, Edward Carlin, John P. Henderson, Elizabeth Johnston, Allan Schmid, James Shaffer, Robert Solo, Henry W. Spiegel, and Paul Strassmann; from several papers written by James F. Becker during the last few years; and from the teaching of the late George John Malanos, who was a wartime student of Joseph Schumpeter's and later provided my earliest knowledge of the man and his ideas.

1. Third edition (New York: Harper & Brothers, 1950). All page references are to this edition.

2. Shortly before his death Schumpeter listed *Capitalism, Socialism, and Democracy* as one of his six most important works (four books and two papers). See Seymour E. Harris, ed., *Schumpeter:*

Social Scientist (Cambridge; Mass.: Harvard University Press, 1951), p. 119. Compare the view of Gottfried Haberler that Schumpeter "regarded it as nothing more than a parergon" (ibid., p. 39). Schumpeter's attention to such "economic sociology" topics as class, leadership, systemic evolution, and so on, date from his earliest teaching years. Schumpeter's interests were much less limited than those of neoclassical economics, although his more technical economic analysis was essentially neoclassical. The Schumpeterian system as a whole is discussed in Richard V. Clemence and Francis S. Doody, *The Schumpeterian System* (Cambridge, Mass.: Addison-Wesley, 1950); Harris, ed., *Schumpeter: Social Scientist;* and Erich Schneider, *Joseph A. Schumpeter* (Lincoln: Bureau of Business Research, University of Nebraska, 1975). The statement in the text may appear extravagant. Certainly, Schumpeter's *Theory of Economic Development* and *Business Cycles* as well as his *History of Economic Analysis* may be similarly described. My point is that *Capitalism, Socialism, and Democracy* treats certain fundamental issues of political economy (or economic sociology, as Schumpeter would say) much more deeply and elaborately than the earlier books. Moreover, his earlier works may be said to reach their capstone in *Capitalism, Socialism, and Democracy*. There is, of course, great continuity in Schumpeter's work; his major analytical books give effect to his early vision. For the view that much of his important later work is "either stated or foreshadowed in his early work," see Harris, ed., *Schumpeter*, p. ix and also pp. 27, 108, 127, and passim.

3. Schumpeter himself practiced reinterpretation to elicit a more intelligible or more correct meaning. See Harris, ed., *Schumpeter*, pp. 103, 113.

4. Compare Herbert von Beckerath, in ibid., pp, 110–118, with Allen M. Sievers, *Revolution, Evolution, and the Economic Order* (Englewood Cliffs, N.J.: Prentice-Hall, 1962), pp. 26–58.

5. Sievers, *Revolution*, pp. 26, 37ff.

6. Veritas Foundation, *Keynes at Harvard* (New York: Veritas Foundation, 1962), pp. 59, 69, 86; 9; 10; 95. Compare Harris, ed., *Schumpeter*, pp. 31–35, 45 n. 76, 113, 115, and 131; on Schumpeter's ideology, see pp. 89–92 and passim.

7. P. 231 n.4.

8. P. 89 n. 4.

9. Pp. 424, 61, 416.

10. P. 416.

11. P. xi.

12. It is difficult to evaluate impartially Schumpeter's attribution of Marx's attractiveness (in part) to envy and (interestingly, in light of subsequent work on Marx's early manuscripts) alienation, that is, to "that feeling of being thwarted and ill treated which is the auto-therapeutic attitude of the unsuccessful many" (p. 6; see also p. 74) and to those "Panting with impatience to have their innings, longing to save the world from something or other, disgusted with textbooks of undescribable tedium, dissatisfied emotionally and intellectually, unable to achieve synthesis by their own effort" (p. 47). The morally denigrating implications of such statements require the antecedent normative premise of the moral superiority of the capitalist (or any other) status quo, whereas Schumpeter also clearly recognized that all social and economic systems were systems of power, and that the quest for power and systemic control characterizes establishment as well as radical persons. Candor apropos ostensible individual motivational pathology thus may be eclipsed by candor apropos systemic reality; perception of one rather than the other will be selective.

Another example: As part of his argument that (contrary to Ludwig von Mises and following Enrico Barone) there can be rational production decisions under socialism, Schumpeter argued that in socialism production and distribution are severed, and the latter is a distinctly political matter (p. 173). But surely the deeper insight—which pervades his book—is that under capitalism also the distributive governance of production (what Schumpeter calls "the distributive automatism of commercial society" [p. 173]) is not utterly devoid of politics (see below).

13. P. 192.

14. P. 77 n. 5.

15. P. 69.

16. Pp. 70, 384.

17. P. 423.

18. P. 170.

19. P. 194.

20. P. 211.

21. Pp. x, 81.

22. P. 171 n. 3.

23. P. 206.

24. P. 243.
25. Chapter 18.
26. Chapter 16.
27. P. 163.
28. P. 75.
29. P. 19.
30. P. 100.
31. P. 55.
32. Pp. 129–130.
33. P. 127.
34. Pp. 142, 196, 206.
35. P. 196.
36. P. 218.
37. P. 284.
38. Pp. 172, 194.
39. Pp. 5–6, 7, 198, 206, and passim.
40. P. 127 and passim.
41. Apropos of "the positivist and rational scholar's tendency in his thinking," see Herbert von Beckerath, in Harris, ed., *Schumpeter*, p. 118.
42. P. 183.
43. P. 271 n. 5.
44. P. 138.
45. P. 51.
46. P. 46.
47. Ibid.
48. P. 54.
49. P. 47.
50. Pp. 64, 107–108.
51. Pp. 64, 69, 70, 154, 156, 198.
52. Pp. 69–71.
53. P. 161 n.5.
54. P. 138.
55. Pp. 56, 50.
56. P. 163.
57. P. 91; see also p. 106.
58. P. 120.
59. P. 140.
60. P. 282.
61. P. 307.

62. Chapter 22.

63. P. 297.

64. Pp. 135, 297–298.

65. Pp. 134–139.

66. Pp. 136, 138.

67. P. 160; see also p. 145.

68. Joseph A. Schumpeter, "The Crisis of the Tax State," *International Economic Papers* 4 (1954), 17. To taxes ought to be added public expenditures.

69. Ibid., p. 19. In his 1927 essay on social classes, Schumpeter wrote: "The bourgeoisie of the first half of the 19th Century established itself in the position gained by its success, created a legal framework to correspond to these successes" (quoted by Wolfgang Stolper in Harris, ed., *Schumpeter*, pp. 107–108; the Bert Hoselitz edition reads: "invested those positions with appropriate legal standing," Joseph A. Schumpeter, *Imperialism and Social Classes* [New York: Meridian Books, 1955], p. 153).

70. P. 167.

71. Ibid.

72. P. 415.

73. P. 169.

74. P. 168.

75. P. 169.

76. P. 197.

77. P. 198.

78. P. 299.

79. P. 197.

80. Pp. 198, 388.

81. Joseph A. Schumpeter, *Ten Great Economists* (New York: Oxford University Press, 1951), p. 217.

82. For example, pp. ix, 143.

83. P. ix.

84. P. 18.

85. P. 124.

86. P. 126.

87. P. 134: see also p. 203.

88. Pp. 126–127.

89. Pp. 134, 131ff.

90. Pp. 13–14.

91. Pp. 145, 160.

92. Pp. 155, 210, 421, and passim.
93. P. 74.
94. Chapters 12, 13, 14.
95. P. 204.
96. Pp. 16, 18, 73, 101, 106, 107, 124, 145, 188, 204, 208.
97. Chapter 14.
98. Bertrand de Jouvenel, *On Power* (Boston: Beacon Press, 1962), p. 177.
99. P. 210.
100. P. 211.
101. P. 215.
102. Ibid.
103. P. 302.
104. Pp. 151, 214.
105. Pp. 216ff., 379, 385–386.
106. P. 355.
107. P. 289.
108. P. 163.
109. P. 162.
110. P. 186.
111. P. 302.
112. Pp. 309–310.
113. Pp 363–366.
114. P. 381.
115. P. 167.
116. P. 72.
117. P. 167.
118. P. 284.
119. Pp. ix, 72ff., chapter 12.
120. p. 417 and passim.
121. Pp. 72, 81, 201.
122. P. 419; see also 157–160.
123. P. 141.
124. P. 73.
125. P. 384.
126. P. 73.
127. P. 139; see also pp. 143, 156, and passim.
128. Apropos Schumpeter and neoclassical economics concerning the concept of capitalism, see Haberler, in Harris, ed., *Schumpeter*, p. 43; apropos capitalism in general, see von Beckerath, in

ibid., p. 117.

129. P. 134 and passim.

130. P. 419.

131. P. 208.

132. P. 156.

133. P. 384.

134. Pp. 170–171.

135. P. 167.

136. Pp. 167–169.

137. Pp. 410, 419, 440.

138. P. 415.

139. P. 167.

140. Chapter 16.

141. Pp. xiii, 162, and passim. In the late 1920s Schumpeter wrote: "Capitalism . . . creates, by rationalizing the human mind, a mentality and a style of life incompatible with its own fundamental conditions, motives and social institutions, and will be changed, although not by economic necessity and probably even at some sacrifice of economic welfare, into *an order of things which it will be merely matter of taste and terminology to call Socialism or not.*" Joseph A. Schumpeter, "The Instability of Capitalism," *Economic Journal* 38 (September 1928), 385–386 (emphasis added).

142. P. 81.

143. P. 156.

144. P. 206.

145. P. 139.

146. P. 219 and passim.

147. See Haberler, in Harris, ed., *Schumpeter*, p. 46 n. 84.

148. See Francis X. Sutton, Seymour E. Harris, Carl Kaysen, and James Tobin, *The American Business Creed* (Cambridge, Mass.: Harvard University Press, 1956); and R. Joseph Monsen, Jr., *Modern American Capitalism* (Boston: Houghton Mifflin, 1963).

149. P. 184 n. 13.

150. John Kenneth Galbraith, *The New Industrial State* (Boston: Houghton Mifflin, 1967).

151. Arthur Selwyn Miller, *The Modern Corporate State* (Westport, Conn.: Greenwood Press, 1976).

152. Charles E. Lindblom, *Politics and Markets* (New York: Basic Books, 1977).

153. Edward S. Herman, *Corporate Control, Corporate Power*

(New York: Cambridge University Press, 1981).

154. Walter Adams, "The Military-Industrial Complex and the New Industrial State," *American Economic Review* 58 (May 1968), 652–665; and *The Structure of the American Economy*, 6th ed. (New York: Macmillan, 1982), chapter 13.

155. John P. Blair, *Economic Concentration* (New York: Harcourt Brace Jovanovich, 1972).

156. Daniel Fusfeld, "The Rise of the Corporate State in America," *Journal of Economic Issues* 6 (March 1972), 1–22.

157. Lindblom, *Politics*, pp. 170ff. and passim.

158. P. 191; see also p. 302.

159. P. 299.

160. P. 293.

161. P. 302.

162. See Sutton et al., *Business Creed*, and Monsen, *American Capitalism*.

163. Compare Richard A. Musgrave and Peggy B. Musgrave, *Public Finance in Theory and Practice* 3rd ed. (New York: McGraw-Hill, 1980), p. 5, with Jesse Burkhead and Jerry Miner, *Public Expenditure* (Chicago: Aldine-Atherton, 1971), pp. 98–99. It is perhaps not irrelevant to note that Schumpeter's position at Harvard was professor of public finance.

164. See Warren J. Samuels, "Normative Premises in Regulatory Theory," *Journal of Post Keynesian Economics* 1 (Fall 1978), 100–114; and "Aspects of Soviet Economic Planning: Power and the Optimal Use of Planning Techniques: A Review Article," *Review of Social Economy* 37 (October 1979), 231–239.

165. P. 310.

166. P. 77 n.5.

167. P. 81.

168. P. 67.

169. Pp. 70, 384.

170. P. 282.

171. *Lansing State Journal*, March 2, 1981, p. A–10.

172. Warren J. Samuels and A. Allan Schmid, *Law and Economics* (Boston: Martinus Nijhoff, 1981).

173. But see chapter 8 and p. 298 n. 8.

174. Thus, for example, macroeconomic policy is influenced by views as to whether upper income persons require more income (and therefore a tax cut) and lower income persons require less income (and therefore cuts in welfare expenditures), to work more;

as to whether unemployment requires cutting wage rates in contrast to recognizing a failure of nerve of businessmen; and as to whether a given decline in productivity is due to routinization or taxation.

175. "*Capitalism, Socialism and Democracy* in particular is full of ironic twists that provide cold comfort for anyone who agrees with him. Capitalists, socialists, and intellectuals are all provided with strong emotional grounds for rejecting the argument." Arthur Smithies, in Harris, ed., *Schumpeter*, p. 16.

176. See, for example, Barrington Moore, Jr., *Injustice: The Social Bases of Obedience and Revolt* (White Plains, N.Y.: M. E. Sharpe, 1978), p. 85.

177. Harris, ed., *Schumpeter*, p. 96 n.24.

178. For example, the work of Gary Becker; contrast the work of Frank H. Knight—both of the Chicago School.

179. For a recent discussion of the general subject, see Robert J. Brym, *Intellectuals and Politics* (Boston: George Allen & Unwin, 1980). For a recent interpretation of the role of the intelligentsia in socialism, see George Konrad and Ivan Szelenyi, *The Intellectuals on the Road to Class Power* (New York: Harcourt Brace Jovanovich, 1979).

180. For example, pp. 81, 264.

181. For example, see Randall Bartlett, *Economic Foundations of Political Power* (New York: Free Press, 1973); Michael H. Best and William E. Connolly, *The Politicized Economy* (Lexington, Mass.: Heath, 1976); Dan Usher, *The Economic Prerequisite to Democracy* (New York: Columbia University Press, 1981); Lindblom, *Politics*; G. Lowell Field and John Higley, *Elitism* (Boston: Routledge & Kegan Paul, 1980); and C. B. Macpherson, *The Real World of Democracy* (New York: Oxford University Press, 1966).

182. Pp. 291, 294.

183. P. 291.

184. Michel Crozier, Samuel P. Huntington, and Joji Watanuki, *The Crisis of Democracy: Report on the Governability of Democracies to the Trilateral Commission* (New York: New York University Press, 1975). See also Holly Sklar, ed., *Trilateralism: The Trilateral Commission and Elite Planning for World Management* (Boston: South End Press, 1980); Herman, *Corporate Control*; and Samuel P. Huntington, *American Politics* (Cambridge, Mass.: Harvard University Press, 1981).

185. See Harris, ed., *Schumpeter*, pp. 118, 130ff.

Pressure Groups and Political Behavior*

Gary S. Becker

I. INTRODUCTION

I first read Joseph Schumpeter's classic, *Capitalism, Socialism, and Democracy*, when a graduate student, and I have recently read it again. I am still impressed by Schumpeter's positive theory of competition for political leadership in democracies. Indeed, his theory stimulated me many years ago to write a paper on the economic approach to political behavior (Becker, 1958, and Becker, 1976b, pp. 31-38). Other parts of the book, however, especially part III, entitled "Can Socialism Work?" were disappointing on rereading. He asks whether the efficient organization of a socialist economy is feasible and argues correctly that this is conceptually possible. He then considers the far more important and difficult question of whether a socialist economy is *likely* to be efficient. His discussion here seems naive, at least after forty years of experience with the Marxist-socialist economies of the Soviet Union, Eastern Europe, and China.

He recognizes that socialist as well as capitalist economies must provide adequate incentives to workers and managers. He apparently believed that weak individual incentives would be compensated by stronger group incentives: "the socialist order presumably will command that moral allegiance which is being increasingly refused to capitalism" (p. 211); "there might be more self-discipline and more group discipline in socialist society, hence less need for authoritarian discipline than there is in a society of fettered capitalism" (p. 212), and "the vested interest in social unrest may be expected to disappear in part" (p. 213), and "*socialism might be the only means of restoring social discipline*" (p. 215; italics in original). He also argued that socialist managers can more readily discipline workers because workers can be deprived of *all* employment by dismissal. He even claimed that "Intellectuals as a group will no longer be hostile" (p. 215), and that trade unions will develop "into exponents of the social interest and into tools of discipline and performance, acquiring an attitude so completely different from that which is associated with trade unions in capitalist countries" (p. 216). This is supposed to describe trade unions in the Soviet Union! And what about the Solidarity movement?

Of course, Schumpeter wrote before most of the evidence about the Soviet Union was readily available in the West. It is far harder to excuse visitors to China in the early seventies, including eminent economists, who returned after brief and highly selective tours with glowing reports about the decline of selfish behavior and the growth of altruistic concern for the well-being of China. The available evidence now clearly indicates that Mao-inspired efforts to eliminate selfish incentives were a dismal failure, and that the Chinese economy (and society!) performed poorly between 1958 and 1977.

Contrary to Schumpeter, I believe that selfish pressure groups of workers, managers, intellectuals, etc., have an incentive to be more rather than less active under socialism (of course, their activities have been forcibly curtailed in Communist countries), because a much larger fraction of resources is controlled by the state under socialism than under capitalism. Nevertheless, because he called attention to the role of competition in the political sector, I would like to believe that Schumpeter would approve of the analysis in this paper of competition among pressure groups for political influence. He might even agree, with the benefit of hindsight, that selfish pressure groups also compete in socialist societies.

The economic approach to political behavior assumes that actual political choices are determined by the efforts of individuals and groups to further their own interests. Most applications of the economic approach emphasize voters, politicians, bureaucrats, and political parties (see Schumpeter, 1947; Downs, 1957; Buchanan and Tullock, 1962; Riker, 1962, and Niskanen, 1971). However, the pioneering book by Bentley (1908) at the turn of the century used an "economic approach" that focused on political pressure groups,[1] and his book led to a large literature by political scientists on the pluralistic society (see, e.g., Truman, 1971). Although Bentley provides an excellent framework for the analysis of political behavior, he does not use it to determine which groups are likely to acquire substantial political influence. This paper uses Bentley's framework to develop a formal model that does generate a number of significant propositions about political influence.

Individuals belong to particular groups—defined by occupation, industry, income, geography, age, and other characteristics—that are assumed to use political influence to enhance the well-being of their members. Competition among these pressure groups for political influence determines the equilibrium structure of taxes, subsidies, and other political favors.

Political influence is not simply fixed by the political process, but can be expanded by expenditures of time and money on campaign contributions, political advertising, and in other ways that exert political pressure. Political equilibrium has the property that all groups maximize their incomes by spending their optimal amount on political pressure, given the productivity of their expenditures, and the behavior of other groups. For analytical convenience, each group is assumed to act as if expenditures by other groups are unaffected by changes in its own expenditures.

Taxes and subsidies are related by the identity between revenue and expenditures: The total amount raised from taxes, including hidden taxes like inflation, equals the total amount available for subsidies, including hidden subsidies like restrictions on entry into an industry. This government budget equation implies that a change in the influence of any group that affects its taxes and subsidies must affect the subsidies and taxes, and hence the influence, of other groups. Therefore, groups do not entirely win or lose the competition for political influence because even heavily taxed groups can raise their influence and cut their taxes by additional expenditures on political activities. This contrasts with the all-or-nothing outcomes implied by many other formal models of political behavior, where the "majority" clearly wins and the "minority" clearly loses.

The distortions in the use of resources induced by different taxes and subsidies, usually called deadweight costs, have a major effect on the competition for influence. Deadweight costs stimulate efforts by taxed groups to lower taxes, but discourage efforts by subsidized groups to raise subsidies. The favorable effect of costs on the political activities of taxed groups gives these groups an "intrinsic" advantage in the competition for influence that presumably is offset by other advantages of groups obtaining large subsidies (see the discussion in section IV).

The analysis in this paper is not limited to taxes and subsidies that distort incentives and reduce aggregate efficiency. The same analysis of competition among pressure groups—without the introduction of social welfare functions or a benevolent government—explains expenditures on defense and other public goods, taxes on pollution, and other government activities that raise efficiency, even when some groups are hurt by these activities. A unified approach is possible because whereas groups harmed by activities that reduce efficiency have the "intrinsic" advantage in the competition for influence, groups benefitting from activities that raise efficiency have the "intrinsic" advantage relative to groups harmed by these activities (see section IV).

II. POLITICAL INFLUENCE FUNCTIONS

The basic assumption of the analysis is that taxes, subsidies, regulations, and other political instruments are used to raise the welfare of more influential pressure groups. Groups compete within the context of rules that translate expenditures on political pressure into political influence and access to political resources. These rules may be embodied in political constitutions or other political procedures, including perhaps "rules" about the use of force to seize power.

To simplify the analysis without any significant loss in generality, I assume that the utility of each person is measured by his real full income, and that full incomes can be added to measure aggregate income or aggregate output.[2] Full income is a better measure of utility than market income because it depends on the time spent at leisure and other nonmarket activities. Envy and altruism are excluded by the assumption that full income depends only on own commodities.

Assume initially only two *homogeneous* groups in the society, s and t. Since identical persons must have the same income, Z_s^0 and Z_t^0 can measure the full income of each member of s and t prior to government redistribution, and Z_s and Z_t their incomes after redistribution, so that

$$R_s = Z_s - Z_s^0 \text{ and } R_t = Z_t^0 - Z_t \tag{1}$$

are the redistributions to each s and away from each t.

All political activities that raise the income of a group will be considered a subsidy to that group, and all activities that lower incomes will be considered a tax. The amount raised by all taxes on t can be written as

$$S = n_t F(R_t), \tag{2}$$

where n_t is the number of members of t, R_t the taxes paid by each member, and the function F, the revenue from a tax of R_t, incorporates the deadweight costs that result from the distorting effects of taxes on hours worked, investments, and other taxpayer choices. Since these costs tend to increase as the rate of taxation increases (see Harberger, 1971 for a good discussion),

$$F(R_t) \leq R_t,\ F' \leq 1, \text{ and } F'' \leq 0. \tag{3}$$

$F(R_t) = R_t$, $F' = 1$, and $F'' = 0$ when taxes do not distort behavior; that is, when "lump-sum" taxes are used.

The subsidy to each member of s is determined from

$$n_s G(R_s) = S = n_t F(R_t), \tag{4}$$

where n_s is the number of members, R_s the subsidy to each member, and G, the cost of providing R_s, incorporates the deadweight costs from the distorting effects of subsidies on hours worked, investments, and other choices by recipients. The properties of G are

$$G(R_s) \geq R_s,\ G' \geq 1, \text{ and } G'' \geq 0. \tag{5}$$

$G(R_s) = R_s$, $G' = 1$, and $G'' = 0$ when subsidies do not distort behavior; that is when "lump-sum" subsidies are used. Equation (4) gives the budget equation between the amount paid in taxes and the amount received as subsidies, a relation that has a major effect on the competition for political influence. Note that the budget equation does not state that subsidies ($n_s R_s$) equal taxes ($n_t R_t$) because deadweight costs reduce subsidies below taxes.

Very different methods have been used to choose legislatures and government officials, to limit the powers of heads of state, and to provide for political succession. All political systems, however, including dictatorial as well as democratic systems, have been subject to pressures from special interest groups that try to use influence to enhance their welfare. I will not try to model how different political systems translate the activities of pressure groups into political influence. Instead, I deal with the end product of such a translation, called "influence functions," that relate subsidies and taxes to the pressures exerted by all groups and to other variables. Since only weak restrictions are imposed on these functions, the basic implications of the analysis should be applicable to widely different political systems, including nondemocratic systems, although, of course, the influence of particular groups is often sensitive to the characteristics of a political system.

If a social welfare function depended on the distribution of income and the pressures exerted by different groups, and if social welfare were maximized with feasible taxes and subsidies, groups with greater "worth" (as defined by the welfare function) would be subsidized. Increased pressure by a group would raise its social "worth" and would reduce its taxes or raise its subsidy.

Influence functions that relate taxes and subsidies to pressure and other variables can be considered "reduced forms" of the social welfare function. To the extent that the distribution of income is a minor determinant of taxes and subsidies, influence functions would depend primarily on the pressures exerted by active groups, the approach of this paper. However, to the extent that traditional welfare economics is relevant, influence would be determined primarily by the distribution of income, and pressure groups would be largely irrelevant. A more general analysis that relates political influence to the distribution of income as well as to pressures from active groups could be readily developed by building on the discussion in this paper.

The amount raised in taxes on t is determined by an influence function that depends on the pressure exerted by s and t and other variables:

$$n_t F(R_t) = -I^t(p_s, p_t, x). \tag{6}$$

Similarly, the amount available to subsidize s is determined by an influence function that also depends on political pressures and other variables:

$$n_s G(R_s) = I^s(p_s, p_t, x). \tag{7}$$

The political budget equation in (4) clearly implies that these influence functions cannot be independent because increased influence of s that raised its subsidy must be financed by increased taxes on t, and hence must lower the influence of t. That is,

$$n_t F(R_t) = -I^t \equiv n_s G(R_s) = I^s;$$

or (8)

$$I^s + I^t \equiv 0.$$

Equality between the amount raised in taxes and the amount spent on subsidies implies that *aggregate influence is zero:* increased influence of some groups decreases the influence of others by equal amounts. Therefore the political game modeled in this paper is zero-sum in influence and negative-sum in taxes and subsidies because of deadweight costs.

Differentiation of equation (8) with respect to any variable y gives

$$\frac{\partial I^s}{\partial y} \equiv I^s_y \equiv -\frac{\partial I^t}{\partial y} \equiv -I^t_y. \tag{9}$$

Therefore, if, say, increased pressure by t raised its influence (and thereby lowered its taxes), increased pressure by t would lower the influence (and subsidy) of s:

$$I^t_t > 0 \Rightarrow I^s_t < 0. \tag{10}$$

Moreover, since $I^s_{ts} = I^s_{st}$, if an increase in p_t raised the marginal product of p_s (if $I^s_{st} > 0$), then an increase in p_s would lower the *absolute* value of the marginal effect of p_t on I^s (for then $I^s_t < 0$ and $I^s_{ts} > 0$). Note also that if some characteristics of a group, such as the occupations or ages of members, raises its influence, these characteristics would lower the influence of the other group.

III. COMPETITION AMONG PRESSURE GROUPS

If $R_t > 0$ and $R_s > 0$, s would be considered the winner and t the loser from the political "game" because s is subsidized and t is taxed. The identity of winners and losers and the amounts won and lost are not rigidly determined by the nature of a political system because they are also affected by the political activities of each group. Losers need not passively accept their fate, but can trim their losses and the gains to winners by lobbying, threats, disobedience, migration, and other kinds of political pressure to raise their influence.

Groups compete for political influence by spending time, energy, and money on the production of political pressure. To model this competition, I assume that each group has a function relating its production of pressure to various inputs:

$$p = p(m,n), \text{ where } m = an, \tag{11}$$

and where a are the resources spent per member on maintaining a lobby, attracting favorable votes, issuing pamphlets, contributing to campaign expenditures, cultivating bureaucrats and politicians, and in other ways. Presumably, pressure cannot decrease and generally increases when expenditures (m) increase.

The total effect of an increase in the number of members on the marginal product of political expenditures, with the amount spent per member held constant, is

$$\frac{\partial p_m}{\partial n} = \frac{\partial^2 p}{\partial m \partial n} = a p_{mm} + p_{mn}. \tag{12}$$

The sign of the first term is determined by whether there are increasing or decreasing returns to the scale of expenditures. The second term tends to be negative because of free riding: each person wants to shirk his obligations and impose the cost of producing pressure on other members (see the pioneering study by Olson, 1965). Free riding can be partially controlled by policing behavior, punishing deviant members with ostracism, intimidation, and fines, and by implementing rules for sharing benefits and costs that reduce the incentive to shirk (see, e.g., Groves and Ledyard, 1977, and Tideman and Tullock, 1976). In essence, free riding raises the cost of producing pressure. Therefore, total expenditures on the production of pressure equals the sum of expenditures on direct political activity and on the control of free riding.

The full incomes of each member of s and t net of expenditures on political activities, including expenditures to control free riding, are defined by

$$Z_s = Z_s^0 + R_s - a_s, \text{ and } Z_t = Z_t^0 - R_t - a_t. \qquad (13)$$

Income per member of a politically active group ($a > 0$) is maximized when

$$\frac{dR_s}{da_s} = 1, \text{ and } \frac{dR_t}{da_t} = -1, \qquad (14)$$

and these conditions take account of all expenditures to control free riding. A group would be politically active only if additional pressure raises its influence. The inequalities in (10) imply that pressure by each group reduces the influence of the other group, and thereby partially or fully offsets the effect of pressure by the other group.

The influence and pressure production functions permit a straightforward translation of the optimality conditions for s and t given by equation (14) into political market equilibrium conditions determining expenditures and pressures by both groups. To simplify the analysis, I assume that each group acts as if the pressure exerted by the other group is unaffected by its behavior.[3] Then

$$\frac{dR_s}{da_s} = \frac{1}{n_s G'} \frac{\partial I^s}{\partial p_s} \frac{\partial p_s}{\partial m_s} \frac{\partial m_s}{\partial a_s} = \frac{I^s_s p^s_m}{G'} = 1, \qquad (15)$$

and using equation (9),

$$\frac{dR_t}{da_t} = -\frac{1}{n_t F'} \frac{\partial I^t}{\partial p_t} \frac{\partial p_t}{\partial m_t} \frac{\partial m_t}{\partial a_t} = \frac{I^s_t p^t_m}{F'} = -1.^4 \qquad (16)$$

These conditions can be solved for equilibrium values of a_s and a_t, and p_s and p_t. They can also be used to derive the effect on the optimal pressure by one group of a given change in the pressure by the other group. Rising deadweight losses from taxes and subsidies ($F'' < 0$ and $G'' > 0$) causes the optimal pressure by one group to increase when pressure by the other is raised (see the discussion in the next section). "Complementarity" in the influence function of *s* between *s* and *t* ($I^s_{st} > 0$) also increases the optimal pressure by *s* when pressure by *t* is raised, because additional pressure by *s* would then be more effective. However, such "complementarity" reduces the optimal pressure by *t* when pressure by *s* is raised, because the negative effect on I^s is reduced.

Comparative static properties of the political equilibrium will be derived graphically, with rigorous proofs given in Becker, 1982. Figure 1 assumes that the reaction curves of both *s* and *t* are positively sloped, because deadweight costs rise sufficiently rapidly as taxes and subsidies increase to dominate any offsetting effects from "substitutability" in the influence functions. Stable equilibrium is implied by the assumption in this figure that *t*'s reaction curve is steeper than *s*'s curve.[5]

Figure 1: Reaction Curves of t and s

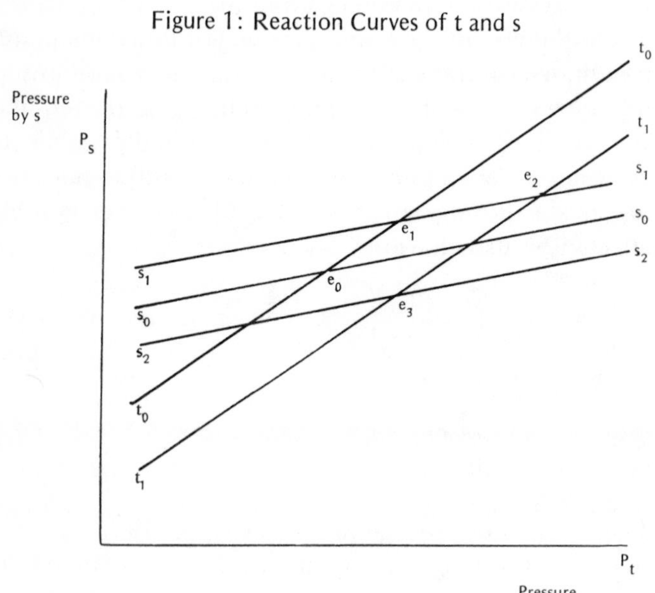

If a group became more efficient at producing pressure, perhaps because of greater success at controlling free riding or at using television and other media, its optimal production of pressure would be raised for any level of pressure by the other group. For example, the reaction curve of s would be shifted upward in figure 1 from s_0s_0 to s_1s_1, and the equilibrium position changed from e_0 to e_1. Pressure by s would necessarily increase, and pressure by t would also increase if its reaction curve were positively sloped. Regardless of the induced effect on pressure by t, the subsidy to s and the tax on t would be increased by an upward shift in s's reaction curve.

This straightforward result applies equally to improved efficiency by t, and will be stated as

Proposition 1: A group that becomes more efficient at producing political pressure will be able to reduce its taxes or raise its subsidy.

If an increase in the efficiency of producing pressure of both s and t shifted the reaction curve of s upward and that of t to the right, the equilibrium pressures of both groups would increase (say, from e_0 to e_2). The influence of either group, however, and hence taxes and subsidies, might not change much, if at all, because the increased pressure by t would offset the increased pressure by s. Recall that the political budget equation implies that both groups cannot increase their influence because aggregate influence is zero (see equation [8]). This illustrates an important corollary to Proposition 1 that has been neglected in discussions of pressure groups.

Corollary: The political effectiveness of a group is determined not by its absolute efficiency—e.g., its absolute skill at controlling free riding—but by this relative to the efficiency of other groups.[6]

For example, a group may be highly subsidized even though it cannot control free riding very well because it has much better control than other groups. Therefore, the emphasis on free riding in many discussions of the effectiveness of pressure groups is a little excessive, because political success is determined by relative, not absolute, degree of control over free riding.

Since economies of scale are important at low levels of expenditure on producing pressure, and since free riding is more easily controlled in small groups, a modest increase in the size of small groups would usually raise the marginal product of their expenditures because the benefit from a larger scale would exceed the cost from greater free riding. Continued expansion in size would eventually cause a decline in marginal products because free riding would become troublesome and scale economies unimportant. Beyond some point, marginal products may stabilize because further increases in size induce little additional scale effects or free riding (per member).

An increase in the size of a group lowers marginal deadweight costs of subsidies or taxes (G' or F') because the subsidy or tax on each member of the group would be reduced. Therefore, the total effect of an increase in the size of a group on its influence depends on the effects on efficiency, subsidies, and deadweight costs. To determine this, it is necessary to consider how deadweight costs affect pressure, taxes, and subsidies.

IV. DEADWEIGHT COSTS AND REDISTRIBUTION

An increase in the marginal deadweight cost of taxes (a reduction in F' in equation [16]) raises the pressure exerted by taxpayers, essentially because a reduction in taxes then has a smaller (adverse) effect on the revenue from taxation. On the other hand, an increase in the marginal deadweight cost of subsidies (an increase in G' in equation [15]) reduces the pressure exerted by recipients, because a given increase in the subsidy then requires a larger increase in tax revenue.

Hence an exogenous increase in the deadweight cost of both taxes and subsidies would shift the reaction curves of t and s to the right and downward, respectively, and change the equilibrium position from e_0 to e_3 in figure 1. Either the equilibrium pressure of t must increase, or the pressure of s must decrease, or both. However, the following proposition holds, regardless of the exact effects on pressure.

Proposition 2: An increase in deadweight cost reduces the equilibrium subsidy.

The cost of many programs, such as agricultural price supports or oil entitlements, has often seemed distressingly large. Yet this proposition implies that politically successful programs are "cheap" relative to the millions of programs that are too costly to muster enough political support,[7] where "cheap" and "expensive" refer to marginal deadweight costs, not to the size of taxes and subsidies.

Since deadweight costs encourage pressure by taxpayers and discourage pressure by recipients, taxpayers have an "intrinsic" advantage in influencing political outcome. For, combine equations (15) and (16) to get

$$-\frac{dR_s/da_s}{dR_t/da_t} = -\frac{I^s_s p^s_m}{I^s_t p^t_m}\,\frac{F'}{G'}. \tag{17}$$

If s and t were the same size ($n_s = n_t$), equally efficient at producing pressure ($p^s_m = p^t_m$ when $m_s = m_t$ and $n_s = n_t$), and equally important in the influence function ($I^s_s = -I^s_t$ when $p_s = p_t$), then (17) would imply

$$\frac{-dR_s/da_s}{dR_t/da_t} = \frac{F'}{G'} \text{ when } p_s = p_t. \tag{18}$$

The "intrinsic" advantage of taxpayers is measured by the right-hand side of (18) and increases as deadweight costs of taxes and subsidies increase—as F' falls and G' rises. There is no advantage with lump-sum taxes and subsidies, because then $F' = G' = 1$. Subsidized groups can overcome their "intrinsic" disadvantage with an optimal size, efficiency at producing pressure, success at converting pressure into influence, or with characteristics that raise their influence. Indeed, the presumption must be that heavily subsidized groups, such as sugar growers and dairy farmers in the United States, not only can redistribute with relatively low deadweight cost, but also can overcome their "intrinsic" disadvantage with political appeal and efficiency.

Proposition 2 implies some "tyranny of the status quo" because the political sector would not interfere much with the private distribution of income even when groups benefitting from interference are better organized. Consequently, the importance of the private status quo does not imply that politicians are lackeys of the rich and is even consistent with the poor being *more* successful politically.

This tyranny of the status quo is not the same, however, as laissez faire, because the political sector would protect the status quo against many shocks and changes in the private sector. Suppose that an industry (autos) pays much higher wages than are available to its employees elsewhere (because they have invested in industry-specific capital) until unexpected competition from imports (Japan) reduces equilibrium wages in the industry below those available elsewhere. If government assistance were not forthcoming, workers would leave the industry and suffer a large reduction in earnings.

Tariffs or quotas on these imports might raise earnings by much more than the loss in consumer surplus and efficiency. For example, if earnings initially were 50 percent higher than available elsewhere, and if they would become 5 percent lower, a complete banning of imports would cost society only 10 percent (5/50) of the subsidy to workers (neglecting the consumer surplus from the increased consumption of autos induced by the lower price of imports). These workers may be able to exert influence and elicit political support because the deadweight cost of doing so is cheap relative to that of other programs.

A well-known maxim of economics states that "sunk costs

are sunk," that individuals look only to the future as they allocate labor and other resources. Without government assistance, even large investments in industry-specific capital would not deter exit from the industry if imports reduced earnings below those available elsewhere. "Sunk costs are not sunk" in the political sector, however, because investments in human or physical capital specific to a firm, industry, or even region reduce the short-run elasticity of supply, and the deadweight costs of "distortions" are lower when supply (and demand) is less elastic. Many persons have been annoyed by the recent political support to Chrysler, because the earnings of their workers had been so high. My analysis suggests that, annoying or not, this may be precisely the reason that Chrysler has been supported.

Political protection against changes in the private sector is likely to be incomplete and temporary. Incomplete because the marginal deadweight cost of protection rises as the degree of protection increases; temporary because supply (and demand) becomes more elastic over time as specific investments depreciate. Therefore, one explanation for periodic efforts at "deregulation," such as the recent deregulation of airlines and securities markets, and to a lesser extent of trucking, is that deadweight costs rise as the duration of regulations increases. A study by Jarrell (1982) indicates that the deregulation of the securities market appears to have been induced by the growth of large institutional traders with elastic demands.

Economists have traditionally explained political behavior, not by the power of interest groups, but by market "failure." Governments produce public goods, reduce externalities, and overcome other failures. Although these political activities raise rather than lower aggregate efficiency, they can be readily incorporated into the previous analysis of competition among pressure groups for political influence.

Activities that benefit all groups are opposed by none and may be actively supported by pressure from some of the groups. More challenging to the analysis are activities that also raise efficiency but harm some groups (say t) who may exert pressure in opposition. The "tax" on t would still finance the "subsidy" to s according to the political budget equation in (4), except that now efficiency would be raised because $n_s R_s > n_t R_t$. If efficiency were also raised at the margin—that is, if $n_s dR_s > n_t dR_t$— subsidized groups have the "intrinsic" advantage in influencing political outcomes, for equation (18) implies that s has the "intrinsic" advantage when $F' > G'$, which is the necessary and sufficient condition for an increase in the subsidy to raise efficiency.[8]

Subsidized groups with an intrinsic advantage exert more pressure than taxed groups of the same size, efficiency, and political appeal. Since political policies strongly supported by pressure from subsidized groups are likely to win out in the competition against other policies, those policies raising efficiency are likely to win unless the groups harmed offset their intrinsic disadvantage with efficient production of pressure or in other ways. This result can be stated as a corollary to Proposition 2:

Corollary: Political policies that raise efficiency are more likely to be adopted than policies that lower efficiency.

This corollary indicates that the model in this paper of competition among political pressure groups to enhance their own welfare does not neglect market failures. That is, the model does not emphasize political redistribution of income at the expense of political increases in efficiency, even though groups do not cooperate and side payments are not permitted. Therefore, an analysis of noncooperative competition among pressure groups can unify the view that governments correct market failures and what has seemed to be a contrary view that governments favor the politically powerful.

Since an increase in the number of persons taxed reduces the tax required on each person to obtain a given revenue and thereby reduces the marginal (and total) deadweight cost of taxation, an increase in the number of taxpayers would reduce their production of pressure. This is why a group would prefer its subsidy to be financed by small taxes on many persons, even when that does not reduce the political efficiency of the taxed groups.[9] The optimal size of a subsidized group is smaller than its most efficient size because an increase in the number of members reduces the net income per member if efficiency does not significantly increase.[10] These results can be stated as:

> *Proposition 3*: Politically successful groups tend to be small relative to the size of the groups taxed to pay their subsidies.

Proposition 3 appears to be consistent with the evidence for agriculture in different countries: Agriculture is often heavily subsidized when a small sector, as in Japan, Israel, or the United States, and heavily taxed when a large sector, as in Poland, China, Thailand, or Nigeria (see Peterson, 1979, and especially the evidence for Africa in Bates, 1981). Proposition 3 and this evidence for agriculture are contrary to the frequent view that small groups are at a disadvantage politically because they do not have many votes. I argue elsewhere (Becker, 1982) that voting and majorities are not the *fundamental* determinants of political influence even in democracies.

I have taken as given the method used to subsidize or tax each group, although usually many methods are possible and the political sector must choose among them. Does competition among pressure groups as modeled in this paper imply that the most efficient method is used? To simplify the discussion of this question, assume that one method of taxation or subsidization is uniformly more efficient than other methods: that $F^* > F$ and $G^* < G$, and $F^{*\prime} > F'$ and $G^{*\prime} < G'$, for all R_t and R_s, where F and G refer to any other method.[11] If influence functions were independent of the tax method in the sense that tax revenue is the same with different methods when pressures by s and t are given,[12] then replacement of a less efficient by a more efficient tax reduces the optimal pressure by *t* because the marginal deadweight loss decreases. This reduction in pressure raises the subsidy to *s* as well as the net income of *t*.

Therefore, both *t* and *s* would lobby and otherwise exert political pressure in favor of the most efficient method of taxing *t* (assuming that the method of subsidizing is unaffected) because both groups are better off with the efficient method. This important result can be stated as

Proposition 4: Competition among pressure groups favors efficient methods of taxation.

If all subsidy methods also yield the same tax revenue when pressures are given, replacement of a less efficient by a more efficient subsidy would raise the subsidy to *s* at the initial equilibrium. Since the marginal deadweight loss from any method increases as the subsidy increases, the marginal loss at the initial equilibrium might be larger with the more efficient than with the initial, less efficient, method. If it were larger, the optimal pressure by *s*, and hence tax revenue, would be reduced, and *t* as well as *s* would be made better off by the more efficient method. Both groups would then favor efficient methods of subsidizing *s* (assuming that the method of taxing *t* does not become less efficient). If, however, more efficient methods induced greater pressure by *s*, tax revenue would increase and *t* would be made worse off by efficient subsidies.[13]

Consequently, noncooperative competition among pressure groups for political influence sometimes, but not necessarily always, favors efficient subsidies. This conclusion may mollify persons who believe that inefficient taxes and subsidies are often used; for example, that a steeply progressive income tax is an inefficient provider of revenue, that the inflation tax should be replaced with consumption or other more efficient taxes, or that aid to farmers and the railroad industry would be provided more efficiently by direct subsidies rather than by restrictions on acreage or on competition from trucks.

Yet a progressive income tax may harm the rich as well as raise revenue, and direct subsidies to farmers encourages entry that can dissipate the gain to established farmers. Indeed, Bruce Gardner has shown nicely (1981) that acreage restrictions are *more* efficient than output subsidies at raising the incomes of established farmers when the supply of farmers is elastic.

Still another example is the evidence that public enterprises are less efficient than private enterprises producing the same products (evidence from many studies is ably reviewed by Borcherding, 1982). Public enterprises often subsidize employees,[14] customers, or suppliers, as well as produce various products. If public ownership is an efficient way to subsidize these groups, replacement of public by seemingly more efficient private enterprises could lower rather than raise *aggregate* efficiency because less efficient subsidies must be used. Consequently, public enterprises may only *appear* to be less efficient than private enterprises, because intentional subsidies are not included in the definition of "output." This and the previous examples illustrate some difficulties in evaluating the efficiency of the public sector, difficulties ignored by numerous casual evaluations.

Expenditures on the production of pressure are not Pareto optimal, because all groups could be made better off by reduced expenditures. Since the influence indifference curves shown in figure 2 are positively inclined because greater pressure by one group lowers the influence of the other group, reduced pressure by both groups could maintain their influence and hence would raise both their net incomes by economizing on political expenditures.

Cooperation among pressure groups is necessary to prevent the wasteful expenditures on political pressure that result from the competition for influence. Various laws and political rules may well be the result of cooperation to reduce political expenditures, including restrictions on campaign contributions and the outside earnings of Congressmen, the regulation and monitoring of lobbying organizations, and

Figure 2: Influence Indifference Curves

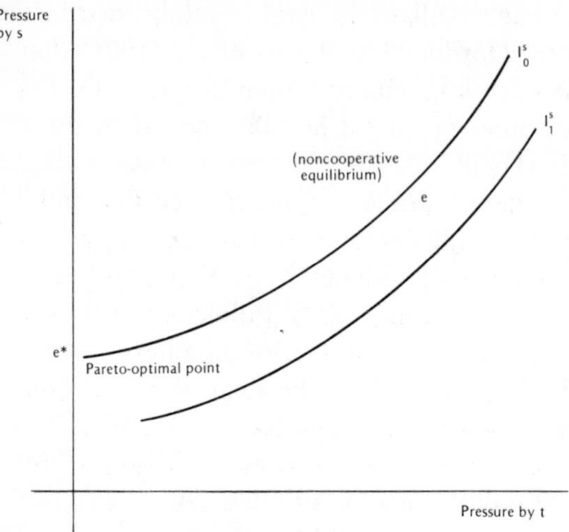

legislative and executive rules of thumb that anticipate (and thereby reduce) the production of pressure by various groups. Cooperation is difficult, however, because each group wants other groups to reduce their pressure and tries to evade restrictions on its own efforts.

V. CONCLUDING REMARKS

Let me conclude by returning to Schumpeter's *Capitalism, Socialism, and Democracy*. Schumpeter believed that capitalism was doomed, not by failure, but by succeeding too well in raising living standards and in providing leisure and freedom for intellectuals and others. Intellectuals use leisure time and opportunities for free expression to undermine capitalism by their hostility and by encouraging the opposition of workers and others.

Intellectuals may well form effective pressure groups that seek research grants and subsidies to cultural and other intellectual activities. They might even seek radical changes in the economic system in the hope of becoming more powerful. Still, I believe that Schumpeter greatly exaggerated the role of intellectuals in subverting capitalism. The analysis in this paper suggests that laissez-faire capitalism is undermined by the efforts of many pressure groups, intellectuals forming a small subset of these groups, to further their own interests by using the power of the state to redistribute resources; various subsidies, taxes, quotas, monopolies, regulations, etc., are introduced to aid some groups at the expense of others. If such redistributive political activities become sufficiently extensive, the resulting economic system is not easily categorized as "capitalistic."

I do not believe, however, that capitalism is especially vulnerable to pressure groups.[15] The political influence of pressure groups undermines not only "pure" capitalist systems but also "pure" socialist and other systems. Indeed, systems in which the state controls a large part of economic life are surely apt to be *more* vulnerable to the demands of powerful pressure groups. Of course, the pressure groups that are powerful under socialism may be quite different from those that are powerful under capitalism. In particular, intellectuals may be less "subversive" under socialism, although I have expressed my belief that they are not a major "subversive" force under capitalism.

Political pressure groups can form more easily in democratic systems, whether capitalist or socialist, than in totalitarian systems. I would substitute a definition of democracy as free competition among pressure groups for political favors in place of Schumpeter's definition of democracy as free competition for political leadership. In democracies so defined, a few pressure groups cannot easily obtain very large subsidies (although many groups may each obtain relatively small subsidies), since I have shown that large subsidies stimulate countervailing pressure by those taxed to finance the subsidies. In totalitarian systems, on the other hand, a few groups can more readily use the state to raise substantially their well-being because other groups are not permitted to form effective opposition. I believe that the major differences between the redistributive activities of democratic and totalitarian political systems can be understood only by understanding the differences between these systems in the amount and nature of the competition among pressure groups for political favors.

NOTES

* Much of this paper is taken from a longer paper, "A Theory of Competition Among Pressure Groups for Political Influence." Center for the Study of the Economy and the State, University of Chicago, 1982.

1. Bentley stated his views forcefully: "Pressure . . . is always a group phenomenon. It indicates the push and resistance between groups. The balance of this group pressure *is* the existing state of society. Pressure is broad enough to include . . . from battle and riot to abstract reasoning and sensitive morality" (1908, pp. 258–260; italics in original).

2. Full income can be added without ambiguity if there is a single household commodity, or if relative prices of different commodities are the same to all persons (see the discussion of full income in Becker, 1981, chapters 1 and 4).

3. Cournot-Nash models of competition among pressure groups are also considered by Brock and Magee (1975, 1978), briefly by Stigler (1975), and by Findlay and Wellisz (1981).

4. Second-order conditions insuring that (15) provides an optimal value of a_s and (16) an optimal value of a_t are considered in Becker, 1981. Sufficient conditions are $I_{ss}^s < 0$, $I_{tt}^s > 0$, and p_{mm}^s and $p_{mm}^t \leq 0$.

5. This assumption is strongly satisfied when $I_{st}^s = I_{ts}^t = F'' = G'' = 0$ because then *s*'s reaction curve would be horizontal and *t*'s would be vertical.

6. I am indebted to Rodney Smith for stressing this corollary.

7. I made this point earlier (Becker, 1976a) without analyzing how deadweight costs affect pressure groups.

8. Since

$$n_s G(R_s) = n_t F(R_t),$$

then

$$G' n_s dR_s = F' n_t dR_t,$$

and

$$n_s dR_s > n_t dR_t \text{ if, and only if, } G' < F'.$$

9. Many persons have argued that subsidies are more readily acquired when each taxpayer is only slightly affected, but the emphasis has been on the cost of organizing taxpayers. An early statement can be found in Simon Newcomb: "If Congress can be induced to adopt a certain policy . . . [a company] can collect an extra profit of one cent per annum out of each inhabitant of the country. Not one person in a thousand would give a moment's attention to the wrong, or indeed ever find it out. Even if he found it out, . . . [h]e could not send a letter, or print a handbill, or call a meeting of his neighbors without spending more time than the question was worth" (1886, p. 457, n. 9).

Pareto said, "If a certain measure A is the cause of the loss of one franc to each of a thousand persons, and of a thousand franc gain to one individual, the latter will expend a great deal of energy, whereas the former will resist weakly" (1971, p. 379).

10. Assume that G has a constant elasticity ($\beta > 1$) with respect to R_s, I^s a constant elasticity ($\gamma < 1$) with respect to p_s, and that p_s has a constant elasticity (α) with respect to m_s and does not directly depend on n_s (no free riding). Equation (15) then implies that the equilibrium values of R_s and a_s change by the same proportion ($=$ to $\frac{\alpha\gamma - 1}{\beta - \alpha\gamma}$) as n_s increases and p_t is held constant. Therefore, if $\alpha \leq 1$, both R_s and a_s, and hence the net income per member, would fall as the number of members increased (even without free riding). However, if $\alpha > 1$ because of economies of scale, net income per member would rise as n_s increased if $\alpha > 1/\gamma$ (without free riding).

11. Note that no method may be *uniformly* most efficient, because methods with relatively large fixed (collection?) costs and small effects on incentives are not efficient at low tax or subsidy levels, and may be efficient at high levels. This point has been stressed in correspondence from Geoffrey Brennan and James

Buchanan; see also Brennan and Buchanan, 1980.

12. An alternative assumption with similar implications is that taxes (R_t) rather than tax revenue would be the same with different methods when pressures are given.

13. If different methods of subsidizing *s* yielded the same subsidy rather than the same tax revenue for given pressure by *s* and *t*, pressure by *s* would always increase when a more efficient replaced a less efficient subsidy. Although the subsidy would increase, tax revenue might decrease, because more efficient methods yield a larger subsidy from a given revenue. The welfare of *t* would be positively related to the tax revenue.

14. For example, public sanitation workers and public transit workers apparently are better paid than private workers (see Edwards and Edwards, 1981, and Pashigian, 1973).

15. Samuelson (See Heertje, 1981, p. 19) appears to believe that capitalism is especially vulnerable.

BIBLIOGRAPHY

Bates, Robert H. 1981. *Markets and States in Tropical Africa.* Berkeley, Ca.: University of California Press.

Becker, Gary S. 1958. "Competition and Democracy." *Journal of Law and Economics* 1: 105–109.

______. 1976a. "Comment" (on Peltzman 1976). *Journal of Law and Economics* 19:245–248.

______. 1976b. *The Economic Approach to Human Behavior.* Chicago: University of Chicago Press.

______. 1982. "A Theory of Competition among Pressure Groups for Political Influence." Center for the Study of the Economy and the State, University of Chicago.

Bentley, Arthur F. 1908. *The Process of Government.* Chicago: University of Chicago Press.

Borcherding, Thomas E. 1982. "Toward a Positive Theory of Public Sector Supply Arrangements." In *Public Enterprise in Canada*, ed. R. Prichard, Toronto: Butterworth.

Brennan, Geoffrey, and Buchanan, James M. 1980. *The Power to Tax.* Cambridge: Cambridge University Press.

Brock, William A., and Magee, Stephen P. 1975. "The Economics of Pork-Barrel Politics." Center for Mathematical Studies in

Business Economics Report 7511, University of Chicago.

______, and ______. 1978. "The Economics of Special Interest Politics: The Case of the Tariff." *American Economic Review* 68: 246–250.

Buchanan, James M., and Tullock, Gordon. 1962. *The Calculus of Consent*. Ann Arbor: University of Michigan Press.

Downs, Anthony. 1957. *An Economic Theory of Democracy*. New York: Harper & Row.

Edwards, Linda N., and Edwards, Franklin R., 1981. "Public Unions, Local Government Structure and the Compensation of Municipal Sanitation Workers." Unpublished manuscript, Queens College, September.

Findlay, Ronald, and Wellisz, Stanislaw. 1981. "Endogenous Tariffs, the Political Economy of Trade Restrictions and Welfare." National Bureau of Economic Research Conference Paper No. 114.

Gardner, Bruce L. 1981. "Efficient Redistribution in Agricultural Commodity Markets." Center for the Study of the Economy and the State Working Paper No. 20, University of Chicago.

Groves, Theodore, and Ledyard, John. 1977. "Optimal Allocation of Public Goods: A Solution to the 'Free Rider' Problem." *Econometrica* 45: 783–809.

Harberger, Arnold C. 1971. "Three Basic Postulates for Applied Welfare Economics: An Interpretative Essay." *Journal of Economic Literature* 9:785–797.

Heertje, A., ed. 1981. *Schumpeter's Vision*. New York: Praeger.

Jarrell, Gregg A. 1982. "Change at the Exchange." Unpublished manuscript, University of Chicago, June.

Newcomb, Simon. 1886. *Principles of Political Economy*. New York: Harper & Brothers.

Niskanen, William A. 1971. *Bureaucracy and Representative Government*. Chicago: Aldine.

Olson, Mancur, Jr. 1965. *The Logic of Collective Action*. Cambridge, Mass.: Harvard University Press.

Pareto, Vilfredo. *Manual of Political Economy*. 1971. Trans. Ann S. Schwier, ed. Ann S. Schwier and Alfred N. Page. (New York: Augustus M. Kelley.

Pashigian, B. Peter. 1973. "Public versus Private Ownership: Consequences and Determinants of Public Ownership of Local Transit Systems." Unpublished memorandum, University of

Chicago.

Peterson, Willis L. 1979. "International Farm Prices and the Social Cost of Cheap Food Policies." *American Journal of Agricultural Economics* 61:13–21.

Riker, William H. 1962. *The Theory of Political Coalitions*. New Haven, Conn.: Yale University Press.

Schumpeter, Joseph A. 1947. *Capitalism, Socialism, and Democracy*. 2nd ed. New York: Harper & Brothers.

Stigler, George J. 1975. *The Citizen and the State*. Chicago: University of Chicago Press.

Tideman, T. Nicolaus, and Tullock, Gordon. 1975. "A New and Superior Process for Making Social Choices." *Journal of Political Economy* 84:1145–1159.

Truman, David B. 1971. *The Governmental Process*. 2nd ed. New York: Knopf.

State Structures and Political Practices:

A Reconsideration of the Liberal Democratic Conception of Politics and Accountability

Samuel Bowles

I. INTRODUCTION

By a common but unfortunate usage in contemporary political theory, politics refers to both an activity and a structure. Political *activity* is often said to be the contest for power, while the political *arena* is the state.[1] Politics, or political activity, then, is one of many distinct practices, distinguished by its object: power. The political arena, or the state, by contrast is one of many distinct sets of rules imparting regularity to practices.

It might seem that the dual usage of the word *political* reflects no more than a semantic awkwardness on the part of social theorists. That we regularly use the word *football* or *chess* to denote both a set of rules and an activity seems inconsequential enough. For politics this is not the case. The designation of both the structure and the practice as political reflects two quite substantive theoretical positions: *the state conception of politics* and the *political conception of the state*. The state conception of politics limits the object of political theory to practices in the state arena: politics is what goes on in the state. The political conception of the state limits the object of the study of the state to politics: what goes on in the state is politics. This essay is a critique of the state conception of politics and two of its component principles: the instrumental view of political practices and the representation of the structure of civil society as contractual.

The instrumental view of politics treats interests or preferences as determined independently of political practices. Politics then is reduced to the mobilization of resources toward the satisfaction of these pre-political interests—or as it is often defined, the study of "who gets what, when, and how." In opposition to the instrumental view, we will propose a constitutive conception of politics: political practices include the creation, preservation, and destruction of the forms of bonding upon which both community and identity are based.[2] The constitutive conception of politics could be termed the study of "who gets to be what, why and when," or simply the *politics of becoming*, in contradistinction to the *politics of getting*.

The second component principle of the state conception of politics, the view of civil society as contractual, represents the structures which regulate practices outside the state sphere as either voluntary exchange relations ("the economy") or as natural (in some formulations, the family).[3] By this reasoning, which we shall investigate further, empirical relations of power in civil society—men over women, capitalist over worker—must be based on either choice or nature, and hence cannot be termed *social domination*. According to this view, where power is to be had it is not there by social contrivance, and where socially contrived advantage is to be had, it cannot be the fruits of the contest for power. Thus the contest for power, and hence politics, is confined to the state. In opposition to the contractual representation of civil society we propose a conception of both family and capitalist production as socially contrived structures assigning power differentially to men and women and to owners and workers. Contests over the rules governing practices in the family, capitalist production, the state, and the interaction of these three structures comprise what we call political practices.

Debates concerning the specificity of the political and the boundaries of the state have a venerable lineage in political theory. Whatever novelty may be claimed for our approach resides in our manner of distinguishing practices from structures and in the resulting distinction between politics and the state.

First, we have adopted a structural theory of power, according to which electoral competition is no more "political" than a discourse or a set of markets. Like elections, markets and discourses exhibit the attribute sometimes thought to define the political: they represent a set of systematic rules regulating social action in a comprehensive or public manner.[4] The effects of language or markets on people—facilitating some projects and excluding others—may, of course, be deemed "private" or "impersonal," unlike the imperatives of the state, some of which take the form of commands carrying the force of law. Yet where socially contrived constraint is demonstrably present what argument can be offered for elevating the "personalness" of constraint to the defining characteristic of power?

Second, a structure is simply any set of rules which regulates and regularizes practices and their interaction.[5] Structures take both organizational and discursive forms. A structure—the state, the family—is not distinguished by what is done there but by how what is done there is regulated. In this, structures are quite analogous to languages, which are distinguished by their rules (of syntax, grammar, etc.), not by the content of conversations conducted in the language. The structures relevant to a study of politics will vary according to the purposes, place, and time of the investigation. We have designated three sites of social practice, each defined by a distinct structure: the state, characterized by the liberal democratic constitution; the family, characterized by a kinship-, gender-, and age-related structure; and capitalist production, characterized by private ownership of the means of production, wage labor, and generalized markets in commodities.

Third, even the "impersonal" structural imperatives of the market or of language must be acted upon to attain force. Structures limit but they do not act. Thus power must be exercised; it must take the form of a practice.

Fourth, we define politics as a practice whose object is the transformation or stabilization of those rules (forms of organization and discourse) which define the family, the state, and capitalist production.

Fifth, because forms of discourse are importantly involved in the rules regulating practices in the state, the family, and capitalist production, a prevalent form of political practice is contestation over language, broadly conceived. We call this form of political practice constitutive politics. Other practices, less central to our argument here, are appropriative (the transformation of nature) and distributive (the transformation or consolidation of access to the products of appropriative practices and other desired social objects and states). The politics of getting is a distributive practice.

Our argument for a constitutive view of political practices, for a political representation of civil society, and against the state conception of politics will demonstrate two propositions. First, the state conception of politics (along with its instrumentalism and contractual conception of civil society) is the source of several inconsistencies in liberal social theory. Second, the resulting lack of coherence cannot be dismissed as a mere anomaly awaiting the progress of normal science, as any attempt to repair the fault will undermine a central claim of contemporary liberal theory, namely that in capitalist societies, the liberal democratic state secures the accountability of power.

The inconsistencies in liberal social theory that we shall demonstrate do not stem from any recalcitrance of the real world to conform to the liberal assumptions of perfect competition in markets and the scrupulous observance of liberal democratic procedural canons in the state arena. Our demonstration concerns the idealized model of market and electoral competition uncomplicated by monopoly, collusion, the de facto suppression of civil liberties, and the circumvention of electoral procedures. Our strategy of argument may be adequately justified by the simplicity and power of an immanent critique; but it is motivated at least as much by the recent forceful advocacy of competitive markets and the depoliticized economy as a coherent model for late capitalist societies.[6]

It might be thought that Marxian social theory would provide the basis for an alternative conception of politics, the state, and democracy less prone to the incoherence of the liberal *corpus*. The Marxian insistence on representing capitalist production as a class relationship only partly encompassed by contractual relations certainly provides the basis for a political view of civil society. And the familiar Marxian dictum that people are produced through their encounters with their social and physical surroundings would seem to invite a constitutive conception of politics. Indeed the work of Gramsci, Habermas, Colletti, Poulantzas, and others has made important steps in this direction. Yet many of the shortcomings of the Marxian critique of liberal democracy may be traced to the very same state conception of politics which plagues the coherence of the liberal theory itself. Perhaps of greater consequence, the state conception of politics continues to inhibit the development of a coherent and compelling socialist conception of democracy.

We will develop the above arguments as follows. In section II we will explore the relationship of the state conception of politics to liberal democratic theory. In section III and IV we will explore the contradictions associated with the contractual conception of civil society and the instrumental view of politics, respectively. In section V we will demonstrate that if the contractual conception of civil society and the instrumental conception of politics cannot be sustained, important claims concerning the accountability of power said to characterize liberal democratic capitalism must be jettisoned. Section VI presents a brief consideration of the state conception of politics in Marxian theory and a sketch of an alternative conceptual framework which may avoid some of the shortcomings of both Marxian and liberal social theory.

II. THE LIBERAL DEMOCRATIC ARGUMENT

We will begin by tracing the emergence and evolution of the state conception of politics. We do not do this to identify our definition of the state conception of politics with any particular writer. (None would subscribe to it exactly, and some great liberal thinkers, J. S. Mill, for example, would take vociferous exception to some parts.) It will be clear, moreover, that our formulation of the state conception of politics is relatively consistent and unified, a status which the underlying arguments did not attain until well into the nineteenth century. Our construction of the liberal democratic argument is far from artificial, however, as we can show that rejection of either the instrumental conception of politics or the contractual view of society casts doubt on the boundaries between private and public so essential to liberal arguments for both liberty and the limited state. Moreover, the roots of the state conception of politics can be traced quite directly to the originators of liberal political theory.

The instrumental conception of politics and the contractual representation of civil society first received systematic articulation in the seventeenth century. They form an integral part of the still dominant answer to what may be termed the Grand Question of Liberal Theory: how is it possible to develop a set of institutions which will allow for the rational coordination of the social division of labor and which are at the same time compatible with a nonabsolutist state.[7] The question was born of the promise of economic progress and nurtured in the shadow of the dual specters of absolutism and popular upheaval. The liberal answer bespeaks a profound pessimism about the possibility of collective choice. The eventually resulting theoretical edifice, which we term the liberal democratic argument, is not so much a system of collective decision making (democratic or otherwise) as a system which purports to do away with all but a bare minimum of collective choice.

The formulation of a compelling answer to the Grand Question awaited two major theoretical developments. The first was the definition of politics as the pursuit of interests, coupled with a theory of interest which was individual, private, and asocial—the political analogue to the concept of conscience in religious thought (to which it was historically indebted). In this development Hobbes's writings, and later Bentham's, constitute the decisive departures, although the earlier contributions of Marsiglio and Machiavelli (who liberated politics from religion) and Luther (who did the reverse) are significant.[8] The magnitude of Hobbes's departure may be seen by contrast to either classical or medieval political theory, in which politics was seen as an aspect of the pursuit of a socially defined good. The later development of the concept of ordinal utility—which denied the possibility of interpersonal utility comparisons—completed the development of an asocial conception of interest.[9]

The second step was the liberation of economics from politics, accomplished through the elaboration of a model of civil society as governed by the exchange of titles to a quite special kind of property (called, appropriately, private) through the medium of markets. This move comprises two reductions; first the economy is reduced to exchange relations, and then civil society is reduced to the economy. Because market exchanges are by definition entered into voluntarily by parties with formally equal recourse to the courts and other agencies of the state, neither the personal interaction of exchange nor the resulting structure of prices can be said to represent a form of unaccountable and socially contrived constraint. Robert Nozick's view is representative:

> There is no central distribution, no person or group entitled to control all the resources, jointly deciding how they are to be doled out. What each person gets, he gets from others who give it to him in exchange for something, or as a gift. In a free society, diverse persons control different resources, and new holdings arise out of the voluntary exchanges and actions of persons. . . . The total result is the product of many individual decisions which the different individuals involved are entitled to make.[10]

Though the origins of the contractual view of civil society are to be found in Locke, its most celebrated and highly developed form is twentieth-century neoclassical economics. Indeed the neoclassical approach goes somewhat beyond Locke and his contemporaries, who distinguished between the wage employment of "servants" and other relations of exchange. As long as such a distinction was made, it might be entertained that the employment relation involves a direct exercise of power by employers over workers.

As early as 1895, however, Wicksell observed that under assumptions necessary to the coherence of the neoclassical economic model the marginal productivity theory of factor pricing and distribution made no use of the fact that the decision maker and the owner of capital were generally the same person. Nothing would be altered, Wicksell ingeniously showed, by supposing that the landlord rented the machines rather than the capitalist renting the land.[11]

The point, of course, was not about landlords. "In competitive model markets," Samuelson wrote half a century later, "it makes no difference whether the capitalist hires the worker or the other way around." Or more generally, according to Lerner: "Economics has earned the title queen of the social sciences by choosing as its domain solved political problems."[12] Lerner goes on to observe that what would appear in other domains as a conflict is represented in neoclassical economics as a contract.

The result, and this is what justifies the liberal designation of property as private, is the apparent divorce of property and power.[13] Thus while the estate of a Russian noble as late as the nineteenth century could be measured indifferently in acres or in souls, and in many European languages the word *landlord* (e.g., *padrone*) means equally boss, or head of household, liberal social thought restricts the relation between property and power to the question of the influence of the wealthy over the state and to the effect of wealth on the feasible scope of market-mediated consumption choices.

While neoclassical economics could demonstrate the irrelevance of power in the relationship of worker to capitalist, the relationship of citizen to the state was irredeemably one of potential domination. Thus questions of the accountability of power came to focus upon the state. The liberal democratic argument, which had always embraced some form of representation, came in the nineteenth century to advocate universal suffrage.[14]

The liberal democratic argument was not quite complete, however, for while the sole locus of power was thus rendered accountable (at least under ideal conditions) and the contractual nature of civil society assured, one could still believe, as Louis Dumont has pointed out, that the social consequences of allocating resources according to the dictates of self-regarding private property and markets are sufficiently undesirable to warrant the systematic and ubiquitous intervention of the state in its operations.[15] This belief would not so much question the privateness of civil society as destroy the boundary between it and the state. The normative acceptability of a contractual view of civil society was buttressed by two quite distinct arguments. According to the first, which acquired its popular force by a rather strained analogy between the privacy of religious conscience and the inviolability of private property, the contractual conception of civil society was justified on the basis of a theory of natural rights. But as state interventions in civil society became increasingly necessary to the reproduction of its structure, a more flexible and hence durable argument based on the putative desirability of the social consequences of these arrangements was developed. The natural rights justification of private property and unregulated markets was progressively jettisoned in favor of a utilitarian defense. This process—which was thought to secure the moral autonomy of economics—was begun by Mandeville (who scandalized his readers), furthered by Quesnay and Smith, and finally fully elaborated by Walras and Pareto.[16]

Our argument will focus on a central claim in the liberal democratic argument: that liberal democratic capitalism ensures the accountability of power. The accountability of power may mean the limitation of power through the defense of negative liberty—"keeping authority at bay" in Isaiah Berlin's phrase—or the positive accountability of power through voting or other mechanisms which constrain the exercise of power to be responsive to the wills of those affected—"popular control over leaders," as Robert Dahl expressed it.[17]

There can be no doubt that the liberal democratic argument is an impressive response to the Grand Question. The question cannot readily be faulted, as the dual problems of the social rationality of labor and the danger of absolutism are as pressing today as they were in the seventeenth century. Nor the response, for no more compelling and fully articulated answer to the Grand Question has yet been developed.[18] But the liberal democratic argument is more heroic than consistent. We will show in our next two sections that the contractual conception of civil society and the instrumental conception of politics underlying these claims cannot be sustained.

III. THE POLITICS OF PRODUCTION

In this section we present our critique of the liberal democratic argument concerning structure. We demonstrate, first, that the representation of civil society as a system of contractual relations is incoherent and, second, that even if the inconsistencies could be rectified, it would be an inadequate basis for the state conception of politics.[19]

We do not wish to claim that exchange and contractual aspects are absent from the social relations of civil society, or even unimportant. Rather, our claim is that the representation of the family and of capitalist production as exchange relations gives rise to substantial contradictions in the theory of capitalist production.

We may begin by exploring the implications of assuming the correctness of the liberal view that production can be adequately represented as a system of contracts. In this case labor would take the form of either "self-employment" or of a service which could be contracted for, not in hours of a worker's time, but in terms of a specific type and amount of work to be done. This contract would be enforceable in that if the specified work were not completed, the purchaser would be under no obligation to pay, or if payment had been made, could recover the payment, if necessary by resort to the courts. Haircuts, babysitting, dentistry, and lawnmowing are common forms of labor services purchased through labor service contracts.

Labor service contracts may be distinguished from *wage labor* contracts. In the wage labor contract, the remuneration is a wage, not a price, and in return for the wage the worker surrenders not a designated amount of labor, but rather formal jurisdiction over a designated amount of his or her time. Piece-rate payment is a combination of a wage labor contract and a labor service contract.

A necessary condition for production is that some labor services be performed. As the wage labor contract does not specify the performance of services, it cannot alone be an adequate representation of the social dimension of any system of production. An adequate representation would have to include specification of the manner in which the employer's formal jurisdiction over the worker's time is translated into a labor service, or in the Marxian terminology, how labor is extracted from labor power.

Thus the liberal conception of a system of production fully characterized by contractual relations must not include the wage labor relationship. But wage labor is the predominant, almost exclusive, form of labor in capitalist societies. Thus if the contractual view of civil society is to apply at all, it must not be to capitalism but to a system of independent or simple commodity production.

Even this application would be unwarranted, however, as can be seen at once if we consider the production of workers (or, more precisely, of labor power). That the production of workers is a necessary aspect of civil society and that this production is regulated by some social structure may hardly be questioned. But can the rules regulating the production of labor power be consistently represented as a set of contractual relations? To see that they cannot, simply observe that the output, labor power, is embedded in people, and hence may be rented, but cannot be owned by anyone but the bearer, except in a slave society. But the owner of the labor power is thus not the producer, or at least is not the decision maker who initiated production. The parent, teacher, or other child rearer transfers skills and appropriate attitudes to a child, who thereby becomes the possessor of labor power. We might wish to characterize this as a gift relationship, or some other form, but it certainly cannot be represented comprehensively as a market exchange or contractual relationship.

We conclude that *if* a system or production of commodities were fully characterized by contractual relations, it would not be capitalist but, rather, simple commodity production; and that *if* relations governing the production of labor power were fully characterized by contractual relations, then the system of production would be based on slave labor.[20]

Not surprisingly, then, the attempt to represent an economy based on wage labor as a system of exchange relations has given rise to a host of anomalies in liberal economic theory. Among these are the difficulty which neoclassical economics has had in explaining (by any but the most *ad hoc* arguments) the compatibility of involuntary unemployment and competitive wage determination, the choice (by presumably cost minimizing employers) of technically inefficient methods of work organization, discriminatory hiring policies which perpetuate wage differences among technically equivalent workers (and which therefore would appear to contradict the requirements of competitive profit maximization) and the structure of salary scales offered by competitive employers which reward both experience and credentials beyond any plausible (much less documented) relationship of these traits to the worker's productivity.[21] In each of these cases, compelling arguments can be made that the anomaly arises from the presumption that all of the relevant relations are contractual, and a resolution of the anomaly can be achieved by taking account of a noncontractual relationship mediating the extraction of labor from labor power.

If our claim that the contractual conception of civil society is inconsistent is conceded, a further implication follows. The presumption that competitive markets achieve normatively attractive (that is, Pareto optimal) results requires that all of the inputs and all of the outputs of the production process be acquired through the exchange of property rights—that is, through markets. The presence of nonmarket interactions—called "spillover effects"—in the production is widely recognized by liberal economists as a source of what is termed "market failure." Debate centers not on the sources but on the extent of these market failures. But when wage labor is employed, market failure is ubiquitous. To see why let us assume that none of the usual external effects exist: all pollution, so to speak, is contracted for. However, labor itself is an input and by the above reasoning unlike labor power cannot be subject to contract. Thus, in any wage-labor-using economy there is no reason to expect competitive market prices to correspond to those which would generate a Pareto optimum. Not to be misunderstood: this argument is quite independent of questions of monopoly, the usual types of externalities, and issues of distributive justice.

We conclude that both the normative and descriptive claims of the contractual representation of civil society must be rejected. Were we to rest our argument here, however, it would be somewhat misleading, as we have focused on the noncontractual and hence direct personal relations of employer to employee and of family member to family member. We have not specified the substantial content of the wage-labor or gender, kinship, and age relationships regulating capitalist production and the production of labor power except to assert that these relationships are governed by distinct sets of rules which are social and that these rules are neither contractual nor electoral. We have not shown that these are relations of domination, but only that models which seem to preclude this are contradictory.[22]

Our argument, however, goes considerably beyond the demonstration that direct relations of domination are not precluded. To see this, imagine a perfectly competitive system of capitalist production. The set of market prices for all goods and labor power in this system, as in any market system, is a set of constraints limiting the actions of the participants. We may illustrate this in a simple choice and constraint situation. An individual consumes both food and concerts. His or her choice of the amount of each reflects the relation of constraints to wants. There is a physical minimum amount of food consistent with survival. We term this the nutrition constraint. Access to both concerts and food is acquired solely by the exchange of property claims at competitively determined prices. Each person's spendable income is determined by the sale of property (including the formal jurisdiction over one's labor power). Given a set of market prices and a set of initial property ownership, this legal and market system describes another constraint, which we term the private property constraint. The private property constraint then states that one's consumption of food and concerts must be such that the total cost of the consumption bundle does not exceed one's income, i.e., goods may not be acquired by theft. Because our argument does not concern distributive justice we may assume that all individuals own the same property, so as to distinguish this point from the familiar and important criticism that voting with your dollars is not an adequate justification of market outcomes because some have more votes than others. Last consider the government constraint, which prohibits more than a certain number of hours of concert attendance per year. The three constraints are depicted in figure 1.

Figure 1: Constrained Choices

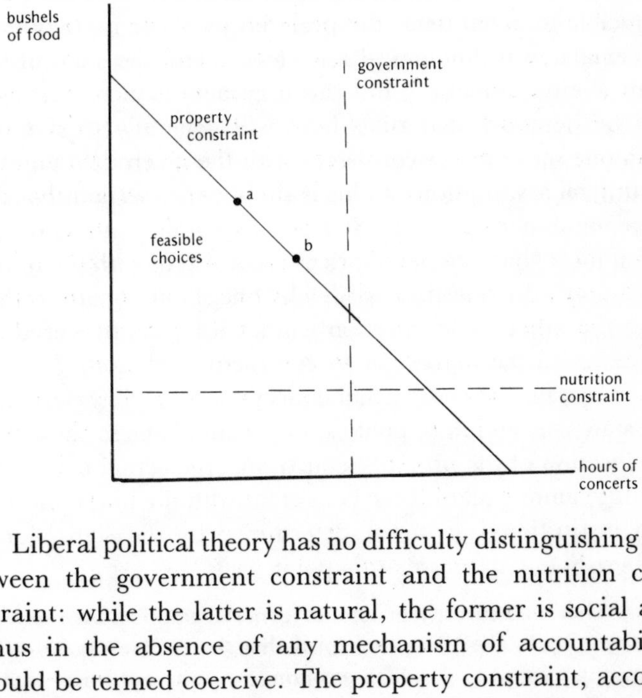

bushels of food
government constraint
property constraint
a
b
feasible choices
nutrition constraint
hours of concerts

Liberal political theory has no difficulty distinguishing between the government constraint and the nutrition constraint: while the latter is natural, the former is social and thus in the absence of any mechanism of accountability could be termed coercive. The property constraint, according to the contractual view of civil society, does not take the form of an interpersonal relation of authority, but it is nonetheless not reducible to a natural constraint. Thus the property constraint is a social contrivance. But the social aspect of the private property constraint, the liberal theory insists, can be limited to the effects of the state and is hence in principle accountable if the state is governed by liberal democratic principles. These state effects on the property constraint are two: the maintenance of the system of private property itself, and any possible effects of the state on the determination of each individual's initial property ownership (through lump-sum taxation, public education, and by other means). All other determinants of the property constraint are then said to be natural.

The argument for this position is as follows: Given a distribution of property and a system of property relations, the prices generated by a set of competitive markets are formally reducible to given data: the preferences of the participants, the available technological knowledge, and the state of the natural environment.[23] But this argument is incorrect, as it can be demonstrated that there will generally exist more than one set of prices consistent with the given data and institutional assumptions. (This is simply an assertion that the price solution is not unique in a general equilibrium model.)[24] But if more than one set of prices is consistent with the initial conditions, the question arises why one should obtain rather than the other. The question cannot itself be answered by reference to the market or to contractual relations.

To sustain the contractual conception of civil society and the state conception of politics, one would have to show that the location of the property constraint (the actual prices obtaining) among all of those consistent with the initial natural and institutional givens is determined by the state alone. Robert Solow expresses this point well:

> What makes the concept of general equilibrium (and its Pareto optimality) so powerful is that the circumstances (constraints) subject to which economic agents optimize—apart from prices and budgets—have to do with technology, tastes, and basic social and legal institutions, all of which are conceived to be fundamentally noneconomic.[25]

But what grounds could be offered for limiting the determination of the actually realized property constraint to the effects of the state? This would amount to reducing the indeterminateness of the economy to a question of state policy or structure, setting aside all nonstate influences on investors' attitudes, conflicts over the intensity of labor, the motivation of workers, and the like. It seems more reasonable to suppose that the actual location of each buyer's property constraint is determined by some presumably complex interaction of the noncontractual elements of civil society and the state with the entire system of production.

This argument demonstrates that the social aspect of the property constraint cannot be reduced to the state, even when preferences, resources, and technology are taken as given. We may thus conclude that the noncontractual relations in civil society exert not only direct personal limiting effects on their participants, but indirect limits via their likely role in the determination of the structure of prices as well.

IV. THE POLITICS OF BECOMING

Having considered the liberal theory of structure (or system) we now turn to a consideration of the theory of practice (or action) expressed by the liberal democratic argument. We will demonstrate that the instrumental conception of politics is inconsistent, and that the model of interests or preferences as determined independently of political practices fails on other grounds as well.

A political theory must include an account of political action, of why people act politically the way they do. But no consistent theory of political action is possible in a model in which political practices are represented simply as instruments toward the satisfaction of exogenously determined preferences. Mancur Olson has shown that as long as the opportunity cost of political activity is not zero, participation in national elections, or in any but small group decision making is generally inconsistent with the instrumentalist conception of the pursuit of exogenously given preferences.[26] The same could be said of obeying the law when the probability of one's transgression being detected is zero. But people do vote in national elections, and obey laws, not only in the pursuit of given ends, but to identify themselves as civic minded, or moral, or whatever.

It will be objected, we suspect, that the law-abiding voter simply has a preference for obeying laws and voting, or for the sense of civic-mindedness or morality thought to result from these activities. This may well be, but it does not save the instrumental model of political practice. Consider whether the behavior of the subject would be affected by a general sentiment that the election was to be rigged, or that the laws in question were issued by an illegitimate authority. The meaning of voting and obeying laws (both to the subject and to those who may observe his or her actions) would thus be altered. So we may conclude that the preference for voting or obeying laws (if this formulation must be followed) is produced by political practices and hence is not exogenous. A far less contorted representation of law-abiding and voting behavior is simply that people act politically both to *get* things and to *be* someone. Because being someone is always a socially constructed objective, preferences must likewise be social rather than individual constructs.

The theory of the politics of becoming goes considerably beyond the assertion that the objectives of political action are socially constructed. The remainder of the argument may be briefly summarized. Individuals engage in intentional activities which alter their own preferences. This process of preference transformation is limited by social constraints. The social aspects of these constraints cannot be reduced to the structure of the state.

Let us consider a person choosing which forms of human development or preference change to engage in. Assuming that he or she has a clear idea of how to develop various wants or capacities for enjoyment, and has some consistent basis for choosing amongst the alternatives, the actual choice will depend in part on the present and expected future prices and other conditions of availability of those goods, services, and social states which are complementary or necessary to the fulfillment of each distinct set of needs.[27]

To illustrate this point let us return to the simple choice model of the previous section. One of the many reasons why the individual might want to attend concerts would be to learn more about music so as to enjoy it more. This motive will of course depend on expected future prices and income, as learning to enjoy music will not be as desirable a project if the expected future price of concerts is prohibitively high. Of course, there may be other social influences on the development of the individual's wants, for example, the extent of government propaganda unfavorable to music. We depict these influences on the individual's choice in figure 2. The locus of points AA describes combinations of government propaganda and future prices which, *ceterus paribus*, would lead the individual to select point a in figure 1. The individual's choice will thus depend on present prices, government prohibitions, government propaganda, and expected future prices. The choice will also depend on the outcome of the individual's prior choices of this type.

Figure 2: Endogenous Preferences

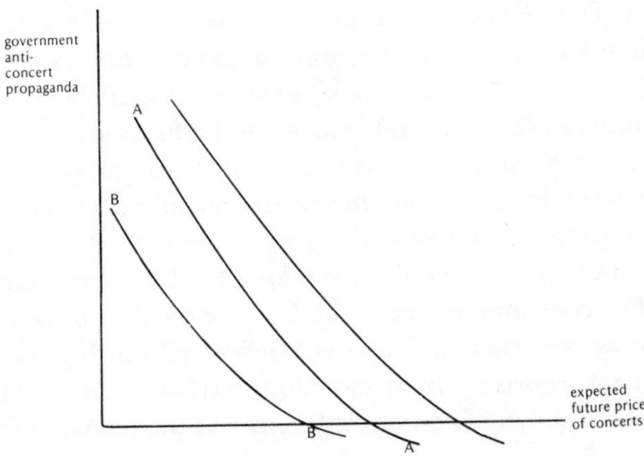

But the price structure, which now appears as a determinant of the evolution of needs or preferences, as we have seen in the previous section, is a social not a natural constraint and one which cannot be reduced to the electorally structured practices of the state. Even in the absence of advertising or other attempts to manipulate others' preferences, therefore, the liberal theory fails to provide compelling reasons for treating preferences as exogenous. Indeed, according to the above argument it would be irrational for people to act as if their tastes were exogenous.

A perfectly analogous argument may be offered concerning language. The forms of development and needs that are expressible or even conceivable are limited (which is not to say determined) by the available discursive tools. Yet the evolution of discourse cannot plausibly be reduced to relations of contract or to the state.[28] Racial insults, the assertion of natural economic rights, combatting pornographic violence, the flag salute, and the evasion of dress codes are nonstate practices which reflect a struggle over discourse, the effects of which may appear in stabilized or transformed patterns of human development and needs.

We conclude that the availability of particular forms of development depends both on prices and discourse and hence on structures whose determination cannot be reduced to the effects of either voluntary exchange relations or the state. The practices relevant to the formation of preferences or interests cannot be plausibly confined to the state arena, or even to the "decision makers" of civil society. Lastly, the resulting needs, norms, loyalties, and affinities are as much the outcome of political practice as their origin. (Or to borrow the language current in political science: preferences are as much an output of politics as an input.)

But the instrumental conception of politics has no theory of the production of people and, as we have seen, will have difficulty erecting one. This is a deficiency which pre-liberal political theorists would have found decisive; for a fundamental concern of earlier traditions was the relation of rules to values, capacities, and community. That the modern liberal tradition has borrowed its language from the lexicon of resource allocation rather than the idiom of human development and community formation, however, does not provide sufficient reason for leaving these concerns to psychologists and moral philosophers. As we shall presently see, even an ahistorical treatment of the accountability claim of the liberal democratic argument returns us directly to the problem of values, capacities, and community.

A further implication concerns J. S. Mill's distinction between the "external relations of the individual" and the "inward domain of consciousness" and "tastes." In the above model, tastes and constraints may still be distinguished, but there is nothing particularly "inward" about tastes, as they are shown to be at least in part the products of "the external relations of the individual." This observation questions the normative status of both negative liberty, which is based on Mill's distinction, and of accountability itself, for it may be wondered what may be said on behalf of the liberty of conscience or the sovereignty of tastes unless the social environment in which the conscience and tastes were formed could itself be justified.

The liberal political theorist might concede, of course, that individuals make choices about their own development, including the development of their wants. It might further be allowed that the determinants of possible forms of human development are social. But it might yet be insisted that in changing themselves people are simply acting on the basis of a system of "metapreferences" (preferences over preferences), which since they are exogenous could then restore the original instrumentalist argument. Attention would then focus upon the social processes determining possible forms of human development. The availability or compulsory status of certain forms of education, the variety of distinct lived experiences open to people, and other influences would then be investigated. Were these directly or indirectly reducible to actions of the state, the argument would have to admit that preferences could not be described as pre-political. The conceptual independence of objectives and constraints, of action and system, and of practice and structure would thus be questioned. But to the extent that the state were governed by liberal democratic rules, one could still argue that both the feasible and the actual patterns of human development were indeed chosen. J.S. Mill, who was more aware than most liberal thinkers of the social construction of needs, developed just such an argument as a defense of liberty. Thus we must explore the claim that the social determinants of tastes are themselves chosen by some accountable procedures.

THE LIBERAL DEMOCRATIC ARGUMENT RECONSIDERED

Let us consider first, what the accountability which is claimed as an attribute of the idealized liberal democratic capitalist model might mean.[29] It may be reduced to the statement that to the extent that individuals' practices are limited by social as opposed to natural constraints, these constraints have either been chosen by the individual or have been determined through some process which may be considered accountable. The "chosen" constraints typically take the form of contracts; the accountability of imposed constraints is typically sought through electoral mechanisms. An accountable process need not be defined except to posit as one of its necessary conditions that it reflect some egalitarian aggregation of individuals' choices. Because preferences are not exogenous and because civil society is not simply a system of contracts, claims of accountability must extend to the formation of wants and encompass not only the state but other structures as well. Thus for the accountability claim to be sustained: the state must be accountable, and *either* the exercise of socially determined power must be absent from civil society, *or* there must be mechanisms for rendering the exercise of power in civil society accountable, either directly or indirectly, presumably through the democratic structure of the state. It is not difficult to demonstrate that none of these statements is true even in the idealized liberal democratic capitalist model.

We have demonstrated already that socially determined power is exercised in civil society. We know of no direct precedures of accountability generally regulating those noncontractual relations which we have identified as the loci of the exercise of socially determined power in civil society—the family and the capital-labor relationship. Thus our argument will concern the accountability of state power and its possible indirect determination of the other structures in which power is exercised.

Our definition of accountability—based on an egalitarian aggregation of people's wants—might seem to pose insuperable difficulties stemming from the conceptual and empirical elusiveness of individual wants. But this is not the case, for if we can show that there are no procedures which might reasonably allow the effective expression and attainment of what people want, we may conclude that peoples' wants (whatever they are) will not be met except by accident. Thus we may avoid the difficult problem of measuring the extent to which wants are actually being met.

More formally, we will argue that the rules which govern practices (including the articulation of practices at the distinct sites) and which regulate the relation of these practices to their effects, diverge in important respects from those rules which would assign a roughly equal weight to each citizen's wants. (It can be seen that this method is perfectly analogous to the demonstration of market failures in the competitive economic model, not by empirically measuring waste, but by demonstrating that the rules governing the allocation of resources systematically diverge from those which would generate a Pareto optimum.)

One of our arguments concerns the rules themselves; the other concerns the terrain over which they are allowed to operate. First, assuming for the moment that formally liberal democratic procedures do allow an egalitarian aggregation of wants, the range of direct applicability of these procedures is severely limited in the liberal democratic capitalist model. Major noncontractual relations—of capital to labor and of men to women—are only tangentially affected by the direct jurisdiction of liberal democratic rules. Workers generally cannot vote out their bosses. No general principles of democratic accountability govern relations between men and women. We have shown in the previous two sections that quite apart from the direct effects of class and gender relations, these nondemocratic relations may indirectly affect choice through their influence on prices and hence on the property constraint and the evolution of wants.

It might be argued that the liberal democratic state has at least potential jurisdiction over family relations and the social relations of production, and for this reason whatever structures regulate social practices outside the state persist only with the implicit consent of the majority. But in the case of the capital-labor relationship, the relationship is more nearly the opposite: the articulation of the social relations of these two sites confers on the owners of capital the power to invest or not, and hence the power to create unemployment or prosperity. Because high levels of employment and economic growth are indispensable to the ability of the leadership of the state to carry out its projects (and indeed even to survive electoral competition) the feasible policies of the state are restricted to those tax laws, educational programs, monetary policies, and the like thought to create a "good investment climate."

The power of the "capital strike"—the refusal of capital to invest unless the climate is right—demonstrates the obstacles to a gradual transition to an alternative system of growth and allocation; but why could not the majority simply vote for an instant and decisive break with capitalism? Assuming that there are viable alternatives to a growth process propelled by private investment, the establishment of a well-working alternative on a scale sufficient to demonstrate its superiority to the majority is a protracted process. In the presence of massive unemployment and economic instability occasioned by a capital strike, movement in this direction may be rejected by the electorate on the grounds of prudence. Thus the broad menu of choices presumed by the notion of accountability requires learning which can only be based on a process of social experimentation which the owners of capital have an ability to discourage out of all proportion to their numbers.[30]

The second reason for doubting the existence or effectiveness of generalized popular accountability is the fact that the responsiveness to majority wants is considerably circumscribed, even in the terrain where the liberal democratic principles formally apply and are not limited by the threat of capital strike. Our argument here affirms James Madison's reassurance to the readers of his celebrated Tenth Federalist Paper that even under "popular government" "a majority . . . included in a fraction" may "be rendered by their number and local situation unable to concert" or "to discover their strength and to act in unison with each other."[31] Like Madison, we assert that "communication and concert result from the form of government itself," though we shall need to extend his reasoning considerably. Thus we argue that in a liberal democratic capitalist society the structures influencing the development of people's capacities, values, and identifications are ill suited to the evolution of a people capable of forming effective majorities and effectively intervening in the formation of policy alternatives and the execution of policy. This is so primarily because the social relations of liberal democratic capitalism inhibit the development of a democratic culture.

By a democratic culture we mean the broadest possible diffusion among the citizens of politically relevant information, skills, and attitudes of political effectiveness, as well as the availability of forms of discourse conducive to the effective functioning of democratic institutions. A frequent claim of the defenders of liberal democratic capitalism is that it promotes precisely such a democratic culture. Nor can these claims, based on arguments dating back to Tocqueville, Jefferson, and Harrington, be summarily dismissed. The discourse of individual rights, the near universal spread of literacy, the extension of social interaction to ever wider circles of contact, the consequent destruction of many forms of parochialism and political deference are all integral to democratic culture, and at least in some measure promoted by the extension of the capitalist relations of production.

Our first two arguments for a critical reconsideration of this view concern the division of labor within the capitalist enterprise and the social division of labor, respectively; our third concerns the structure of liberal discourse itself.

Consider the experience of production as it may affect the formation of people and communities. We do not have to turn to Marx for concern that the organization of the labor process within the capitalist enterprise is antithetical to the production of a democratic culture: Tocqueville, Smith, and even Adam Ferguson, Smith's mentor, foresaw the dangers well before the birth of the Marxian tradition. A modern restatement of the argument may begin by noting that under conditions of capitalist production, the division of labor within the enterprise exhibits four relevant characteristics: the minute fragmentation of tasks, the separation of conception from execution, the hierarchical control of the labor process, and the assignment of persons to positions on the basis of race, sex, age and academic credentials.[32] These four characteristics would appear to promote precisely the opposite of a democratic culture, as they concentrate information, information processing, and decision-making skills at the narrow pinnacle of a pyramidal structure. At the same time the structure of capitalist production promotes a sense of political ineffectiveness and assigns to racial, sexual, and other differences a set of hierarchical meanings which are both inconsistent with tolerance and respect and hostile to the forms of solidarity and cooperation necessary for effective political intervention.[33]

The point is a familiar one, but those who make it often do not provide arguments sufficient to trace these antidemocratic effects to the specifically capitalist structure of production. Indeed, each of the four characteristics above might well be thought to be the lamentable manifestations of the technologically or genetically determined requirements of efficient production which presumably would appear in any system and thus would present natural rather than social limits to accountability. Even more may be claimed, for in the liberal economic model of perfect competition in which labor itself is a commodity, the structure of production must correspond to the most efficient methods. Thus, because "it makes no difference who hires whom," the hierarchical structure of the labor process would be unaffected by any set of social arrangements which maintained a commitment to efficient production. To the extent that the characteristics of the labor process are social rather than natural in origin they correspond to deviations from the putatively efficient competitive equilibrium, perhaps as a result of monopoly.

If labor *were* a commodity and its use was governed simply by contractual relations, the liberal counterclaims would be compelling. But as we have shown in section III, the representation of labor as a commodity is inconsistent. It is precisely the noncontractual aspect of the relationship between wage labor and capital—the extraction of labor from labor power—which simultaneously explains the four above characteristics of the labor process *and* forces a divergence between efficiency and profitability even under competitive conditions. It is on this basis that we can claim that the hierarchical structure of the labor process is consistent with a competitive equilibrium of profit-maximizing, noncolluding capitalists, but it is not reducible to the imperatives of technical efficiency in production. We are thus permitted to say that these characteristics of the division of labor within the enterprise are not the result of technological requirements or genetic limitations (or at least not entirely so) and are (at least in part) the result of the specifically capitalist structure of production even in its idealized competitive form.

If the antidemocratic nature of the labor process has been all but ignored by advocates of the liberal democratic argument, the other facet of the division of labor—the private and decentralized coordination of the activities of the producers of diverse commodities through the medium of markets—has, as we have seen, provided its foundation. It is true, to be sure, that since Tocqueville few liberal theorists have made much of the relationship between markets and culture. Where the issue has been raised, as in Friedman's classic defense of markets, it has been to assert that markets inhibit prejudice, censorship, and the arbitrary use of power. This argument, which as Hirschman has recently pointed out, may be traced back to Montesquieu, is a compelling one.[34] But it is so partial that it is radically misleading. The truth of the argument lies in the anonymity and range of choice offered in markets, which explains, to cite Friedman's example, why the consumer of bread does not care whether it was produced by a Negro, a Jew, or a Communist.[35] The shortcoming of the argument consists in overlooking the competitively imposed structure of the labor process alluded to above and its tendency to reproduce sexism, racism, and other forms of invidious distinction and, perhaps more important, in abstracting from the relationship between markets, political participation, and the formation of a democratic culture.

This second flaw, to the best of our knowledge has been entirely overlooked. The argument is quite straightforward. A democratic culture is produced through the activities which people undertake. Perhaps the most important of these activities is democratic politics itself. J. S. Mill expressed this familiar point:

> this discussion and management of collective interests is the great school of that public spirit, and the great source of that intelligence of public affairs, which are always regarded as the distinctive character of the public of free countries.[36]

Under what conditions will people engage in this "discussion and management of collective interests?" Clearly, where such opportunities exist and where there are incentives to participate. The incentives to participate will be greater where something important is at stake, or to put it differently, where the opportunity cost of not participating is high.

Markets minimize the opportunity cost of not participating in democratic political practices. In this respect markets undermine the production of a democratic culture. This is true for two reasons. First, to the extent that most important social outcomes are generated by market-based allocation processes and to the extent that these processes both formally and substantively circumscribe the effective jurisdiction of democratically constituted decision processes, what is at stake is reduced. Second, markets provide ubiquitous if not complete alternatives to political action as a means towards acquiring desired ends. That markets might undermine democratic political participation through limiting the stakes and reducing the opportunity costs of not participating is perhaps not surprising. For it is precisely this reduction in the "need" for collective decisions which is so much applauded in liberal social theory.

Perhaps an example will make our point clear. Consider the disgruntled parent of an elementary school student seeking to rectify the inadequacy of the curriculum at the neighborhood public school. Assuming that the parent's suggestions have been ignored, she may organize others to elect a new school board, or threaten to do so. Or, she may withdraw her child, cut back on other expenditures if this is possible, and send the child to private school. The opportunities open to the parent are, to adopt Albert Hirschman's terms, voice or exit.[37] Markets inhibit participation by ensuring that the option of exit is always present, thus undercutting the commitment to voice.

The example may appear limited but it is not. The person who feels strongly about street crime or air pollution can either organize to improve the social and physical environment, or he can "shop" for a community with a bundle of characteristics more to his liking. Or if his resources and mobility are limited, he can buy an air conditioner, or a gun. Further, in the example above the availability of a private school is not critical as long as the administration of schools is decentralized and the parent is free (within the limits of the private property constraint) to move (and to buy or rent accommodations) elsewhere.

These effects of the two facets of the division of labor in capitalist production—markets and the hierarchical labor process—are augmented by a third barrier to the evolution of a democratic culture. This is the structure of liberal democratic discourse itself. By couching its fundamental normative and procedural principles in terms of individual rights, liberal democratic discourse makes difficult the expression of solidarity and cooperation as goals of political practices. The only form of community or of bonding recognized in the liberal discourse is nationality, based on common citizenship, and kinship, based on the family. The preeminence of family and nation as viable communities is more than a characteristic of liberal thought—their relative prominence is actively promoted by the virtual destruction of all other communities through the operation of markets in commodities and labor power. It is perhaps for this reason that among the most vibrant forms of the politics of becoming in the U.S. today are nationalism and the antifeminist defense of the patriarchal family. But even a passing acquaintance with the history of the now liberal democratic social formations in the twentieth century, or with the contemporary analysis of authoritarian discourse (or "personality") may suggest the at best ambiguous contribution of family- and nation-based bonding to the formation of a democratic culture. For this reason, appeals to the solidarity and cooperation necessary for the exercise of popular power are ill served by the liberal discourse.

We conclude that the unaccountable determination of the decision to invest, the structure of the labor process, markets and liberal democratic discourse itself render both the determination of the social constraints on choice and the development of wants effectively unaccountable in the liberal democratic capitalist model.

VI. CONCLUSION

The liberal democratic argument is at once a theory of structure, or practice, and of interests. Its theory of structure, we have suggested, is flawed by an inconsistent contractual representation of civil society. Its theory of practice posits an unsupportable conception of political action based on individualistic and pre-given asocial preferences. The resulting theory of interests is rendered vacuous and normatively unappealing by the recognition of the unaccountable social construction of wants and of conscience.

Our critique of the liberal democratic argument has proposed a structural concept of power and a constitutive conception of politics derived from Marx's theory of capitalist production and his critique of political economy. We have simply generalized his claim that people produce themselves in production and that market relations are a partial and hence inadequate representation of the structure of capitalist production.[38] Very much like Marx's opening chapters in volume 1 of *Capital*, we have sought to demonstrate that the formally equal procedures said to characterize liberal society, far from being universal, are quite limited. Like him we have argued that the plausible result of these equal but limited procedures is to confer vastly unequal powers on society's participants. Further we would argue (though we have not done so here) that the liberal democratic structure and interpretation of the vote and the wage relationship contributes in important ways to the illusion of substantive equality and thereby to the reproduction of the underlying relations of power and exploitation. Finally, like Marx, we have identified the noncommodity status of labor, the distinction between labor and labor power, and hence the noncontractual aspects of the wage labor to capital relation as the critical analytical distinction in a critique of liberal thought.

We have extended Marx, of course, by giving sustained attention to the state as an integral component of a capitalist society. In doing this, we have drawn little if at all on Marx's early writings on political theory. Our approach is also quite at odds with important subsequent strands of Marxian thought. We will review three points of difference.

First, if the flaw of the structural basis of liberal democratic theory is to eradicate politics from civil society and thus to reduce politics to the relationship of citizens to the state, many strands of contemporary Marxism, no less than orthodox Marxism, reduce politics to the study of class relations through the materialist determination of the superstructure by the base. Thus the state may be the instrument of the dominant class, or it may be the "vectoral sum" of a "balance of class forces" or it may be the terrain of class struggle, but in the last instance it may not be anything at all in its own right but a reflection (however complex) of class relationships.

This class reductionist theory may be distinguished from ours in that it does not represent the state as a distinct structure governed by distinct rules which are irreducible to the social relations of production (or the imperatives of their reproduction) and whose apparatus is capable under some conditions of becoming a major historical actor as opposed to simply a derivative force.[39] The class reductionist position has had unfortunate consequences for the development of Marxian political theory. A notable result, we believe, is the failure to understand the absolutist state, both in its early modern and contemporary variants, and the confused and inconsistent representation of the postcolonial states of Africa, Asia, and Latin America.[40] Equally important is its associated lack of appreciation of the progressive accomplishment of the liberal attack on absolutism and its inattention to the quite considerable distinction between the liberal state (which espouses liberty but not universal suffrage), and the liberal democratic state. Most serious, perhaps, is the related presumption that with the elimination of classes under communism, the state, the patriarchal family, and all other reflections of class relations will wither away.

Second, a complement of the class reductionist theory of the state is an economistic representation of the social relations of production. This tendency is most prevalent in Marxian economics, where the predominant interpretations of the labor theory of value banish politics from production only slightly less effectively than does neoclassical economics.[41] The result is an isomorphism of structures and practices whereby political practices take place in the state and economic practices take place in the economy. This formulation, which is hardly limited to the structural school, simply repeats the flaw in the state conception of politics.[42]

Third, the usual Marxian concept of objective interests with its twin, false consciousness, cannot be easily reconciled with the principle that people produce themselves through their social practices.[43] Objective interests in the Marxian framework, unlike the preferences of liberal theory, are socially constituted. But they are pre-political in the sense that they can be read directly from the structure of class relations. Thus interests are known, at least by the party or by the theorist, and the task of politics becomes the *realization* of the interests of the working class (or of the majority). According to this view, politics may, like the structure of the state, reflect or express the class structure, but class interests are in no sense the product of political practices, except insofar as those practices alter the class structure itself. It is this instrumentalism which constitutes the line of descent from St. Simon to Lenin (who also thought that politics could be reduced to "the administration of things"). It is not the state but politics that withers away in Leninist thought. In this, the Leninist conception of politics differs little from that of the public administration conception of politics which is characteristic of modern-day elitist social engineering.[44]

The humanist alternative to the orthodox Marxist conception of class-determined objective interests is little different in this respect, for in this formulation interests are equally defined as prior to practices. Common to both formulations is the difficulty (a rather imposing one for those committed to political relevance) in relating present wants and actions to the often quite different "objectively" (genetically or class based) defined interests of the actors.

Marxian political theory thus exhibits many of the difficulties which we have identified in the liberal democratic *corpus*. The shortcomings of the Marxian theory have perhaps been exacerbated by the fact that in recent years the body of Marxian thought has fragmented into three relatively self-contained theories: a theory of interest developed by Marxist humanists, a theory of structure developed both by Marxian economists and other structuralist Marxists, and a theory of practice whose most important exponents are the modern-day Gramscians.

A compelling alternative to the liberal democratic argument—if it is to come from the Marxian tradition at all—must reintegrate the theory of structure, practice, and interests in a manner which avoids the isomorphism of practices and structure, the class reductionism, and the instrumentalism mentioned above. A number of authors have taken promising steps in this direction. Our own suggestions concerning practice and structure were outlined in our introductory section and have been developed in a series of recent papers. Let us here comment briefly on the particularly perplexing and ineradicable problem of interests.

We may begin by distinguishing between procedural and substantive arguments. A substantive argument is defined over outcomes, a procedural argument is defined over the manner in which inputs are processed. Thus Nozick's argument, as cited, is a procedural justification of market-determined income distributions, and Marx's theory of exploitation is a substantive critique of that procedural argument, demonstrating the compatibility of competitive markets and formal legal equality among the exchanging parties with the expropriation of surplus labor time.

The dilemma of the liberal democratic argument concerning interests as a normative basis for democratic political theory is that it must choose between a substantive argument (the state is responsive to what people want) which is flawed by the unaccountable social constitution of wants, and a procedural argument which is flawed by the limited terrain over which the procedures apply.

An analogous dilemma confronts the Marxist critique of the liberal democratic argument. A political analogue to Marx's theory of exploitation requires a substantive critique. This would demonstrate the compatibility of formally equal procedures (universal suffrage and civil liberties) with substantially unequal political outcomes (domination). But can such a political analogue be created? The normative appeal of Marx's theory of exploitation is based on the Lockean presumption that one's just claim on the social product is derived from labor. By measuring labor performed as embodied, socially necessary, abstract labor time, Marx was able to juxtapose the substantive outcome (expropriation of surplus labor time) with the formally equal procedures governing the process. Some have sought the analogue to this theory in the integration of the theory of alienation and the labor theory of value. While the work of Colletti and Macpherson (from quite different perspectives) has developed this line of reasoning, the concept of the expropriation of "subjectivity" or "developmental powers" has remained elusive.[45]

The problem is not one of measurement but of concept. The Marxian theory of exploitation (in its orthodox formulation) relies on an external objective measure of interest: control over labor time. Yet a constitutive theory of politics —to which both Colletti and Macpherson have made significant contributions—would seem to preclude such an approach. If people and groups are not assigned interests behind their backs, so to speak, but constitute them through the interaction of their practices and the relevant structures, the strategy of substantive critique must itself be critically reassessed.

We cannot claim to have developed a satisfactory resolution of the tension occasioned by insisting on both the political production of interests and the necessity of some concept of interests as distinct from the empirical wants that people experience at any given moment. It is a difficult question, and a venerable one. It seems possible, however, that a consistent and appealing argument could be developed by postulating that interests do not reside in relations between people and things (utilitarianism) nor in intrinsic essences (humanism, objective class interests), but in the structure of social relations. The substantivist position, with its tendency, if pursued, to waver between empiricism and essentialism, would thus be rejected in favor of a procedural or more precisely structural argument.

If the concept of interest can neither be identical to felt wants nor determined independently of them, by what structural argument might interests and wants be connected? We may rephrase this question: under what kinds of social relations can wants be said to represent interests? As the former is an empirical concept and the latter normative, the connection cannot escape a normative commitment. Having rejected any intrinsic conception of interests, the normative content of the concept of interests concerns the conditions governing the process of want formation.

A solution to the problem may lie in an extension of the reasoning behind Habermas's concept of an ideal speech situation which would locate the normative content of interests in the democratic and egalitarian social relations which govern the process of want formation. Alternatively, we may say that egalitarian democracy—which would have to be defined as a set of structures—is that set of social arrangements which reconciles want and interest. Because interest here has no specific definition (except that it cannot be unrelated to wants), the normative content of the definition is borne exclusively by its commitment to egalitarian democracy.

This conception of interests shares with many utopias the quest for a society devoid of illusion, whose transparency facilitates popular and reasoned collective decision making. It does not, however, propose an end to history or to structural change, as no arguments have been offered for the fixity of interests. Nor does it imagine that the tension between individual interest and collective rationality may be established by any society, no matter how egalitarian and democratic. Less still does it advocate a leap over history, as its foundation—the democratic politicization of capitalist civil society—is a vision rooted in real historical processes and vibrant social movements which have already left their mark on the twentieth century.[46]

NOTES

* This essay draws upon Herbert Gintis's and my recent critique and reinterpretation of the labor theory of value (Bowles and Gintis, 1981) and represents an application of the basic conceptual framework developed in our forthcoming book on the relationship of economic, political, and cultural concepts in the liberal and Marxian theories. Charles Bright, Jeanne Hahn, Susan Harding, and Robert Paul Wolff helped clarify and develop some of the arguments presented here.

1. Thus Robert Dahl writes, "a political system is any persistent pattern of human relations that involves to a significant extent power, rule, and authority." Dahl, 1963, p. 6. While according to Dahl, families may be considered political systems, for most political scientists the words (and department labels) *government* and *political science* are interchangeable. See also Pateman, 1975.

2. While our concept of constitutive politics differs considerably from Macpherson's notion of the pursuit of developmental powers, our work has been greatly influenced by his writings. See Macpherson, 1973 and 1962, especially. We have also borrowed from Offe, 1980; Unger, 1975; Przeworski, 1977; Fay, 1977.

3. Our treatment of the contractual representation of civil society owes much to Wolin, 1960, and Dumont, 1977.

4. The public nature of a practice, however, is an insufficient basis for its definition as political, as the private-public distinction is irreparably vague, whether either the location of the activity or its consequences are being considered. In this we differ from Wolin, 1960, who writes that questions concerning the responsibility of corporate management or trade union leadership "do not belong to the species of political problems. . . . Political responsibility has meaning only in terms of a general constituency, and no multiplication of fragmentary constituencies will provide a substitute," p. 432. We find the notion of a constituency difficult to define. If it refers to the formal rules of a given structure, it is surely too limiting; but if it is defined in terms of effects it must (given a high level of social interdependence) be so inclusive as to be lacking in specificity (and would certainly include the activities of trade union and corporate leadership).

5. Our concepts of structure and practice are developed in more adequate detail in chapter 2 of our forthcoming book.

6. We are referring, of course, to the resurgence of pre-Keynesian laissez-faire economics in the U.S. and Europe. But our argument is equally directed toward those on the left who have narrowed their critique of liberal democratic capitalism to a matter of distributive justice.

7. Our "Grand Question" is suggested by Ian Gough's Grand Project of Liberalism: the expansion of the forces of production and the perpetuation of representative forms of government.

8. See Skinner, 1978, and Pocock, 1975.

9. It is true, of course, that scarcely had ordinal utility replaced cardinal utility when interpersonal utility comparisons were reintroduced via the mechanisms of the social welfare function.

10. Nozick, 1974, pp. 149–150.

11. Wicksell, 1934.

12. Samuelson, 1971, and Lerner, 1972.

13. Dumont, 1977, has developed this point. He writes that "a clear distinction can be drawn between what we call political and what we call economic" only after "there emerged an autonomous and relatively unified category of wealth." "The factual precondition for our familiar distinction" was the development whereby, citing Landes, 1969, "the ruler abandoned . . . the right or prac-

tice of arbitrary or indefinite disposition of the wealth of his subjects" (p. 6). Dumont has thus insightfully drawn our attention to a critical contribution to the development of liberal and later liberal democratic thought. But Dumont's distinction is not ours, which would insist that in a slave-owning society in which the rights of private property were not transgressed by the state, the liberal separation of politics from economics would be thwarted by the evident integral (not merely empirical) relation of property to power. See also Polanyi, 1944.

14. The contractual interpretation of the wage labor relationship and the arguments for the extension of the suffrage were not merely parallel theoretical developments. As Macpherson's study of the Putney debates has shown, seventeenth-century opposition to the extension of the vote to employees was often based—even among the Levellers—on the interpretation of the wage labor relationship as a surrender of will by the "servant."

15. Dumont, 1977.

16. Hirschman, 1977, also makes this point.

17. Berlin, 1969, p. 126, and Dahl, 1956, p. 3.

18. Lest socialist democrats should despair (or take offense), it should be remembered that none of the more or less comprehensive theoretical structure of the liberal democratic argument was completed until at least a century after the emergence of capitalism as a unified and dominant set of concrete institutions.

19. The ideas presented here are developed in greater detail in Gintis, 1976; Marglin, 1974; Stone, 1974; Edwards, 1979; and Burawoy, 1980.

20. See Bowles and Gintis, 1981.

21. In addition to the works cited in note 19, see Reich, 1981; Roemer, 1979; Bowles, 1981; Bowles and Gintis, 1977.

22. We take this agnostic position for reasons of economy. The presence of domination can be quite readily demonstrated to be a condition for the profitable employment of wage labor, and it would be inferred from the differential access of men and women, workers and owners both to the means of coercion and to the material necessities of life, or from a study of differential life chances, or from a direct study of the political processes of families and corporations, or perhaps, by other methods.

23. A straightforward presentation of this argument is Bator, 1957.

24. This is the upshot of the Cambridge capital controversy. See Harcourt, 1969.

25. Solow, 1979, pp. 340–341.

26. Olson, 1968. Less obvious, perhaps, is the fact that an instrumental and asocial conception of interests is necessary to the proof of Kenneth Arrow's justifiably celebrated impossibility theorem. This dramatic result demonstrates that with ordinal preferences of the type characteristic of neoclassical economic thought, and indeed of all modern utilitarianism, majority rule will under quite general conditions produce intransitive results such that in sequential paired elections, a majority of the electorate might prefer A to B; B to C, and C to A. Yet if preferences are social in the sense that it is meaningful to say "I prefer candidate A over candidate B more than she does," preferences are no longer ordinal in the sense that generated Arrow's troublesome result. (That the Arrow anomaly may be formally resolved through the introduction of interpersonal comparisons of utility does nothing, of course, to provide a concrete electoral mechanism capable of reconciling the principle of majority rule with a concern for varying intensities of preferences. Arrow, 1951.)

27. Gintis, 1974, demonstrates this result rigorously.

28. See Gintis, 1980, for a further elaboration.

29. The claim that liberal democratic capitalism is reproducible (in the sense that the reproduction processes of its defining structures are consistent) may be considered an argument parallel to the accountability claim. We consider the reproducibility claim in Bowles and Gintis, 1978, and Bowles and Gintis, 1982.

30. In 1933 Keynes argued against free trade on the grounds that it would inhibit social experimentation, which he then thought necessary to develop an alternative to capitalism (Keynes, 1933).

31. Madison et al., 1961, p. 20.

32. Braverman, 1974, and Edwards, 1979.

33. This argument is made and considerable empirical support marshalled in Kohn, 1969; Pateman, 1970; Edwards, 1979; and Bowles and Gintis, 1976.

34. Hirschman, 1977.

35. Friedman, 1962.

36. Mill, 1947.

37. Hirschman, 1970.

38. For a related contribution see Wolfe, 1974.

39. However, see the work of Block, 1980.

40. We develop this point in our recent critique of the work of Perry Anderson on the absolutist state. See Gintis and Bowles, 1983.

41. See Bowles and Gintis, 1981.

42. Lenin, for example, wrote that "democracy is a form of the state" and, perhaps more surprisingly, Habermas affirms:

> the modern state can be understood as the result of the differentiation of an economic system which regulates the producton process through the market—that is, in a decentralized and unpolitical manner. The state organizes the conditions under which the citizens . . . carry on the production process. The state itself does not produce. . . .

See Hunt, 1980, p. 15 for the Lenin quote and a critique of this position, and Habermas, 1979, p. 189.

43. See Przeworski, 1977, and Gintis, 1980.

44. Fay, 1977, and Wolin, 1960, develop this point.

45. See Macpherson, 1973 and 1962, and Colletti, 1972.

46. See Bowles and Gintis, 1982.

REFERENCES

Arrow, K. 1951. *Social Choice and Individual Values.* New York: John Wiley & Sons.

Bator, F. 1957. "The Simple Analytics of Utility Maximization." *American Economic Review*, March.

Berlin, Isaiah. 1969. *Four Essays on Liberty.* Oxford: Oxford University Press.

Block, F. 1980. "Beyond Relative Autonomy." *Socialist Register*, pp. 227–242.

Bowles, S. 1981. "Competitive Wage Determination and Involuntary Unemployment." Mimeo, May.

______, and Gintis, H. 1976. *Schooling in Capitalist America.* New York: Basic Books.

______, and ______. 1977. "Heterogeneous Labour and the Marxian Theory of Value." *Cambridge, Journal of Economics* 1/3 (Fall).

______, and ______. 1978. "Have Capitalism and Liberal Democracy Reached a Parting of the Ways?" *American Economic Review*, May.

______, and ______. 1981. "Structure and Practice in the Labor Theory of Value." *Review of Radical Political Economics* 12/4.

______, and ______. 1982. "The Crisis of Liberal Democratic Capitalism." *Politics and Society* 11/1 (Winter).

______, and ______. 1983. "The Power of Capital: On the Inadequacy of the Conception of the Capitalist Economy as Private." *Philosophy Forum*, Summer.

Braverman, H. 1974. *Labor and Monopoly Capital*. New York: Monthly Review Press.

Burawoy, M. 1980. "The Politics of Production and the Production of Politics." *Political Power and Social Theory* 1:261–299.

Colletti, L. 1972. "Bernstein and the Marxism of the Second International." In *From Rousseau to Lenin*. London: New Left Books.

Dahl, Robert. 1956. *A Preface to Democratic Theory*. Chicago: University of Chicago Press.

______. 1963. *Modern Political Analysis*. Englewood Cliffs, N.J.: Prentice-Hall.

Dumont, Louis. 1977. *From Mandeville to Marx*. Chicago: University of Chicago Press.

Edwards, R. 1979. *Contested Terrain*. New York: Basic Books.

Fay, B. 1977. "How People Change Themselves: The Relationship between Critical Theory and Its Audience." In T. Ball, ed., *Political Theory and Praxis*. Minneapolis: University of Minnesota Press.

Friedman, M. 1962. *Capitalism and Freedom*. Chicago: University of Chicago Press.

Gintis, H. 1974. "Welfare Criteria with Endogenous Preferences." *International Economic Review*, June.

______. 1976. "The Nature of the Labor Exchange." *Review of Radical Political Economics*, Summer.

______. 1980. "Theory, Practice, and the Tools of Communicative Discourse." *Socialist Review*, Spring.

______, and Bowles, S. Forthcoming. "State and Class in European Feudalism." In Charles Bright and Susan Harding, eds., *States and State Formation in Europe and America*.

Habermas, J. 1979. *Communication and the Evolution of Society*. London: Heineman.

Harcourt, G. 1969. "Some Cambridge Controversies in the Theory of Capital." *Journal of Economic Literature* 7:369–405.

Hirschman, A. 1970. *Exit, Voice and Loyalty*. Cambridge, Mass.: Harvard University Press.

______. 1977. *The Passions and the Interests*. Princeton, N.J.: Princeton University Press.

Hunt, Alan. ed. 1980. *Marxism and Democracy*. London: Lawrence and Wishart.

Keynes, J. M. 1933. "National Self-Sufficiency." *Yale Review*.

Kohn, M. 1969. *Class and Conformity*. Homewood, Ill.: Dorsey Press.

Lerner, A. 1972. "The Economics and Politics of Consumer Sovereignty." *American Economic Review*, May.

Macpherson, C. B. 1962. *The Political Theory of Possessive Individualism*. Oxford: Oxford University Press.

______. 1973. *Democratic Theory: Essays in Retrieval*. Oxford: Oxford University Press.

Madison, James, et al. 1961. *The Federalist Papers*. New York: Anchor.

Marglin, S. 1974. "What Do Bosses Do? The Origin and Function of Hierarchy in Capitalist Production." *Review of Radical Political Economics* 6/2 (Summer).

Mill, J. S. 1947. *On Liberty*. New York: Appleton-Century-Crofts.

Nozick, Robert. 1974. *Anarchy, State and Utopia*. New York: Basic Books.

Offe, Claus. 1980. "The Emerging Coexistence of Two Paradigms of the Political." Mimeo.

Olson, Mancur. 1965. *The Logic of Collective Action*. Cambridge, Mass.: Harvard University Press.

Pateman, C. 1970. *Participation and Democratic Theory*. Cambridge: Cambridge University Press.

______. 1975. "Sublimation and Reification: Locke, Wolin, and the Liberal Democratic Conception of the Political." *Politics and Society*, pp. 441–467.

Pocock, J. G. A. 1975. *The Machiavellian Moment*. Princeton, N.J.: Princeton University Press.

Polanyi, Karl. 1944. *The Great Transformation*. New York: Farrar & Rinehart.

Przeworski, A. 1977. "Proletariat into Class." *Politics and Society* 7/4, 343–401.

Reich, M. 1981. *Racial Inequality.* Princeton, N.J.: Princeton University Press.

Reomer, J. 1979. "Divide and Conquer: Microeconomic Foundation of the Marxian Theory of Discrimination." *Bell Journal of Economics*, Fall.

Samuelson, P. 1971. "Understanding the Marxian Notion of Exploitation." *Journal of Economic Literature* 9/2, Spring.

Skinner, Q. 1978. *The Foundations of Modern Political Thought.* Cambridge: Cambridge University Press.

Solow, Robert. 1979. "Alternative Approaches to Macro Economic Theory." *Canadian Journal of Economics*, August.

Stone, K. 1974. "The Origin of Job Structures in the Steel Industry" *Review of Radical Political Economics* 6/2.

Unger, Roberto. 1975. *Knowledge and Politics.* New York: Free Press.

Wicksell, K. 1934. *Lectures on Political Economy.* London: Routledge & Kegan Paul.

Wolfe, Alan. 1974. "New Directions in the Marxist Theory of Politics." *Politics and Society* 4/2.

Wolin, Sheldon, 1960. *Politics and Vision.* Boston: Little Brown.